1979

1979

THE YEAR
THAT SHAPED THE
MODERN MIDDLE EAST

DAVID W. LESCH
Trinity University

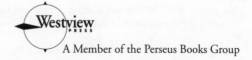

A Member of the Perseus Books Group

Copyright © 2001 by Westview Press, A Member of the Perseus Books Group

Westview Press books are available at special discounts for bulk purchases in the United States by corporations, institutions, and other organizations. For more information, please contact the Special Markets Department at The Perseus Books Group, 11 Cambridge Center, Cambridge MA 02142, or call (617) 252-5298.

Published in 2001 in the United States of America by Westview Press, 5500 Central Avenue, Boulder, Colorado 80301-2877, and in the United Kingdom by Westview Press, 12 Hid's Copse Road, Cumnor Hill, Oxford OX2 9JJ

Find us on the World Wide Web at www.westviewpress.com

Library of Congress Cataloging-in-Publication Data
Lesch, David W.
   1979 : the year that shaped the modern Middle East / David W. Lesch.
   p.   cm.
Includes bibliographical references and index.
ISBN 0-8133-3916-2 (pbk. : alk. paper); ISBN 0-8133-3942-1 (hc)
   1. Middle East—History—1979-   2. Iran—History—Revolution, 1979.
3. Egypt. Treaties, etc. Israel, 1979 Mar. 26.   4. Afghanistan—History—
Soviet occupation, 1979–1989.   I. Title.

DS63.I L47   2001
956.05—dc21

                                                                    2001026657

The paper used in this publication meets the requirements of the American National Standard for Permanence of Paper for Printed Library Materials Z39.48–1984.

10   9   8   7   6   5   4   3   2   1

To my wife, Suzanne, and my son, Michael

CONTENTS

PREFACE

This is, at least for me, a different sort of book. The idea for writing it essentially emanated from three different sources. One was pedagogical. In some of my Middle East history courses over the years, I found myself consistently utilizing the year 1979 as one of the major political, economic, and cultural breaking points in the Middle East in the post–World War II era. Second, I read a book a few years ago by Ray Huang titled *1587, A Year of No Significance: The Ming Dynasty in Decline.*[1] The book is a narrative of typical life during a year in China in which nothing particularly significant happened according to the commonly accepted historical annals. However, in this snapshot treatment, Huang offers clear signs of irreversible decline in the Ming dynasty by examining the breakdown of various aspects of what on the surface would seem to be mundane bureaucratic and pedestrian developments. I then started to imagine the possibility of examining a "year in the life" of the Middle East, albeit one that comprised a number of events that would be deemed significant in any history book. In effect, it is the negative of Huang's snapshot approach. That is, whereas he detailed primarily the mundane, I outline and examine the spectacular. Finally, and maybe most importantly, my first serious interest in Middle East history, politics, and culture was generated while I was an undergraduate student in the late 1970s and early 1980s. The events of 1979 and their direct repercussions in the several years that followed intellectually drew me to this tumultuous region of the world.[2] Maybe this indicates a certain personal bias toward this period of time; however, I would venture to guess that there is a whole generation of Middle East scholars (and policymakers) who might say the same.

This book is relatively compressed, consisting of only four chapters. It is, save for the methodological treatment in Chapter 1, not based on original research. I do not pretend to claim any new profound discoveries regarding the specific events covered in the book. The three foci of the manuscript, that is, the primary events of 1979—the Iranian revolution, the Egyptian-Israeli peace treaty, and the Soviet invasion of Afghanistan—have all been examined in detail by a host of highly qualified scholars and commentators.

What I *am* claiming is that the year 1979 was a watershed in modern Middle East history, and I explain why. I connect the dots of history that in retrospect clearly elevate the Western historical categorization called a solar year, in this case, 1979, to a level that separates it from much of the rest of those historical categorizations called a year. The efficacy and acceptability of attempting this sort of an examination are delineated in the opening introductory chapter. As a historian, I felt obligated to confront this issue head-on and to explicate my rationale and those in other venues. Although this chapter may be a bit technical in terms of history lexicology and methodological interpolation for the nonhistorian, I felt it was necessary to have (or at least put forth) some intellectual underpinning to my historiographical approach and interpretation.

Some may view this book as containing a few peculiarities regarding form and structure. On several occasions I begin a sentence with the representation of a year in its Arabic numeral form rather than spelling it out, which, of course, is grammatically incorrect; however, I did this in order to emphasize that I am focusing upon the events of one particular year and their short- and long-term repercussions.

I also frequently employ the term "annualization," especially in Chapter 1. This term and my variants of it (such as "annualizer") are not listed in any of the *Webster's Dictionary* volumes I own, so I assume they are not generally recognized words. To my knowledge, it has also not been used in any colloquial manner or by another scholar/writer seeking to convey a thought more directly through a word construction that can be somewhat easily digested by the reader yet not be accorded official acceptance. Frankly, I have utilized this term because I could not think of any other that better reflected my methodological approach. It is not "periodization" in its truest form, since I am examining a block of time that has already been compiled and categorized in the appropriate form. What I am doing is choosing from a plethora of convenient historical categories that have come into existence over time—era, millennium, century, score, decade, year; the process of selecting the "year" category I elect to call annualization.

Finally, the book contains only four chapters—and disparate ones at that. The nature of and rationale for Chapter 1 I have briefly outlined above. Since I felt that the general reader may have a limited understanding of modern Middle Eastern history, Chapter 2 consists of a brief overview of the three signal events of 1979: the Iranian revolution, the Egyptian-Israeli peace treaty, and the Soviet invasion of Afghanistan. Chapter 3, "Future Past," is the culmination of my argument; that is, the historical dots are connected. Much of the future that lay ahead of 1979 is now our past. This is why it is considerably longer than the preceding chapters. What I attempt to do is simply let the history flow forward and out from the pages in a "Tarantinoesque" fashion, hopefully making it obvious to the reader the immense importance of the events of 1979 by virtue of the matrix of interconnected and circular repercussions that are still very much with us today. There is no prestidigitation involved—it's "just the facts." In Chapter 4, however, I do offer some general statements about the subject and reflect on the relationship between time, change, and chance in connection with the events under discussion.

To say that the events of 1979 did not in a significant and unalterable manner change the Middle East—indeed, the world—is simply being blind to history. In just the "A" section of an August 2000 issue of a local newspaper were the following stories: Osama bin Laden, from his sanctuary in Afghanistan, reportedly issued a new threat against American interests abroad; a series of bombs exploded in India-controlled Kashmir, with a Pakistani-based Islamist group claiming responsibility; American and British air force jets bombed a couple of suspected anti-aircraft missile sites in the no-fly zone in southern Iraq; the Venezuelan president ignored the international ban on visiting Iraq and met with President Saddam Hussein to discuss OPEC matters, particularly continued price stability and cartel solidarity; PNA President Yasir Arafat, Israeli Prime Minister Ehud Barak, and U.S. officials were feverishly trying to prepare the ground and close the negotiating gaps for a possible second Camp David summit meeting with U.S. President Bill Clinton (after the first one in July failed to produce the desired results); the Lebanese army had finally deployed units in the border zone with Israel following the latter's precipitate withdrawal from south Lebanon a few months earlier; and in Iran, the new reformist president continued his tussle with conservative clerics over the forced closure of pro-reform newspapers. One can trace important strands of all these stories to the events that transpired in 1979.

We are not blind, and it cannot be argued that the events of 1979 did not significantly alter the Middle East. I only hope I do justice to and show the proper respect for such a lively year.

As with any idea that comes to fruition, there were many individuals who nurtured its growth along the way. I especially want to thank Robert O. Freedman, William Quandt, and Steve Yetiv for reading earlier drafts of this book and for the many helpful comments they made that improved the manuscript. In fact, in a rather intellectually stimulating lunch a couple of years ago, Bob Freedman helped me crystallize the ideas I had on the topic for the book; for Bob, it led to a conference he organized in November 2000 on a subject linked to the events of 1979, which will undoubtedly result in one of his typically outstanding edited works. I wish all lunches were so productive! I also want to thank my colleague in the Department of History at Trinity University, John Martin, our resident intellectual historian, for reading over the introductory chapter and suggesting some things that made the argument a bit more cohesive. Others who helped develop my ideas and/or suggested various sources were Jonathan Owen, Char Miller, Bill Udell, and Lou Cantori. Karl Yambert, senior editor at Westview Press, did a marvelous job of getting this book published in a relatively short span of time. It has been a pleasure to work with him on this project. Eunice Herrington, the senior secretary in the Department of History at Trinity University, was, once again, of inestimable help in getting the manuscript into publishable shape and form. Finally, I could not finish a project of any appreciable length without the support of my wife, Suzanne, and my son, Michael, to whom this book is so appropriately dedicated.

David W. Lesch
San Antonio, Texas

Introduction:
The Secular Priesthood
and "Annualization"

Some dates seem mute or virtually inaudible, lost in the white noise of chronology, while others have tremendous resonance and speak volumes.

—John Brewer,
"The Year of Writing Dangerously"

There are certainly many years in modern history that resonate louder than others. In the West, the years 1776, 1789, 1848, 1914, 1945, and 1989 immediately evoke historical images and meanings with just their simple enunciation. There are also a number of individual years in modern Middle East history that "speak volumes." The ledger since the end of World War II would invariably include the following: 1948, 1955, 1956, 1967, 1973, 1982, 1991, and 1993. In each of these years, war, realignment, and/or the establishment of frameworks for peace have occurred; that is, some event or series of events engendered a dramatic and lasting period of change by causing shifts in the balance of power and/or ideological and perceptual transformations in the region that frequently also had extraregional reverberations. However, at no time in the post–World War II era was dramatic and all-encompassing change more apparent in the Middle East than in 1979—so much so that, in my opinion, future Middle East historians and social scientists will conclude that the year 1979 constituted a major watershed, if not *the* major watershed, in modern Middle East history.

To begin to understand the significance of 1979 one only has to review the more noteworthy events that occurred in that year: the culmination of the Iranian revolution in February when Ayatollah Ruhollah Khomeini came to power replacing Muhammad Reza Shah; the signing of the U.S.-brokered Egyptian-Israeli peace treaty in March; the taking of the Grand Mosque in Mecca by Islamist radicals in November (and its bloody end when Saudi troops regained control of the site); the infamous hostage crisis, when Iranian revolutionaries stormed the U.S. embassy in Teheran in November, capturing and holding fifty-two Americans for 444 days until their release in January 1981; and finally, the Soviet invasion of Afghanistan in December.

Although the recognition of the year 1979 as significant might seem obvious, it has not been given anywhere near its proper due or analyzed in its totality. In studies of post-1948 Middle East history, that is, after the creation of the state of Israel, the year 1967 is most often singled out as *the* watershed.[1] This is quite understandable given the fact that the seminal Arab-Israeli war occurred in June of that year with, inter alia, the following results: the creation of the occupied territories situation, with Israel acquiring the Sinai Peninsula and Gaza Strip from Egypt, the West Bank from Jordan, and the Golan Heights from Syria; the establishment of the principle of land for peace, embodied in UN Security Council Resolution 242 passed in November 1967 and, therefore, the basis for a peace process that is still operative today; the effective end of secular Arab nationalism with the convincing defeat of its standard-bearer, Egyptian President Gamal Abd al-Nasser; the resuscitation of Islamism in the wake of the clear ineffectiveness of secular Arab ideologies in confronting Israel and the increasing awareness of the secular Arab regimes' inability to manage their own economies; the intimate involvement of the two superpowers in the Arab-Israeli conflict, a scenario that reached its fruition in the near nuclear confrontation between the United States and the Soviet Union during the latter stages of the 1973 Arab-Israeli war; and the acceleration of political divisions within Israel revolving around the question of how much, if any, of the occupied territories should be returned to the Arabs in exchange for peace.

My contention is not that 1967 should necessarily be replaced as a watershed in post-1948 Middle East history, but that the year 1979 should be accorded at least the same historical recognition. The events that occurred in 1979 fundamentally altered the entire Middle East. A new regional balance (maybe, in view of subsequent history, it would be more appropriate to say imbalance) of power was created; the events of that year deepened the link between the Arab-Israeli and Persian Gulf arenas, a process that began with the 1973 Arab-Israeli war; before then, the two arenas were separate and distinct in the minds of most policymakers, analysts, and scholars. It is also reasonable to suggest that the events of 1979 accelerated (or, indeed, began in earnest) the "balkanization" of the Middle East; that is, there was a return to historical regionalism, where the majority of states in the area began to outwardly pursue policies of national self-interest and/or adhere to subregional groupings. Egypt's decision to make peace with Israel, essentially abandoning the tenets of Arab nationalism for its own professed national interests, epitomized the changing regional landscape.

These events had far-reaching consequences, even more so, in my opinion, than the 1967 Arab-Israeli war. Although many of the significant occurrences in 1979—most obviously the Egyptian-Israeli peace treaty—would not have happened (or certainly not in the fashion they in fact did happen) if not for the 1967 Arab-Israeli war, the 1967 war was essentially the climax of a process that began with the conflictual creation of the state of Israel. It also did not change the direction of this process, as proven by the Arab-Israeli war occurring only six years later that, in essence, completed the military aspect of the Arab-Israeli paradigm in place since 1948. The Egyptian-Israeli peace treaty completed, in large measure, the political and diplomatic strands of the 1948 paradigm and set the Arab-Israeli arena off in a new direction, for better or worse. In addition, the other seminal events of 1979, the Iranian revolution and the Soviet invasion of Afghanistan, affected the Persian Gulf and Central Asian arenas of the Middle East in a direct and overwhelming manner, so that by the end of the year, the elements were in place to effect dramatic change over the entire Middle East and not just primarily in the Arab-Israeli arena. An important breaking point in modern Middle East history had occurred, and a new paradigm had been established. Certainly, the previous one no longer applied. 1979 was both an end and a beginning.

The Examination of One Year

Perhaps the first question to address is why consider just one year and not a block of time. A similar case could be made for the period 1977–1980 instead of just 1979. This would encompass Egyptian President Anwar Sadat's pivotal trip to Israel in November 1977, which set the Egyptian-Israeli peace process in motion, and the Camp David accords in September 1978, which established the framework for peace and accelerated, if not saved, the process. This block of time would also include the bulk of the events that constituted the Iranian revolution, which resulted in the overthrow of the Shah in early 1979, and the political infighting and systemic breakdown in Afghanistan, which necessitated, from the Kremlin's point of view, the Soviet invasion in late 1979. The Iran-Iraq war beginning in September 1980, a major aftereffect of the Iranian revolution, would be factored into the equation. One could also expand the block of time to 1982 to include the Israeli invasion of Lebanon, which, many would say, was at least an indirect result of the Egyptian-Israeli peace treaty.

My view is that the events of 1979 climaxed a series of processes that closed the door on previous interwoven paradigms that had established the parameters of interaction in the Middle East and opened the door to new ones. The culmination or climax of these processes was not at all assured. We know very well from the 1993 Israeli-Palestinian "Oslo" accords signed at the White House that agreeing to peace does not necessarily mean actual peace, especially that which is consecrated by internationally recognized agreements. The Camp David accords facilitated and probably saved the Egyptian-Israeli peace process, but President Jimmy Carter had to personally intercede again in March 1979 in order to prevent it all from falling apart. By the end of 1978, one could conclude that the Shah was likely to be overthrown, but it was not at all inevitable. Until the Shah actually left, and until Ayatollah Khomeini actually secured power, there was no Iranian revolution of which to speak. Success made it one, and it only became successful in February 1979. Revolution is supposed to mean change.

We speak of the Hungarian "uprising" in 1956 or the Prague "spring" in 1968; they are not called revolutions because they were unsuccessful and, therefore, they did not result in revolutionary change. As far as the events that transpired immediately after 1979, such as the Iran-Iraq war and the Israeli invasion of Lebanon, these will be discussed in their proper context, that is, as events resulting from changes wrought by the events of 1979. They do not warrant discussion within the same temporal category as a focal point of change.

There have been a number of books titled with the numerical representation of a particular year, often followed with a subtitle that refers to the significance of that annum. When something is titled with simply a year or some sort of date reference, it usually has overt meaning to a great many people (or at least the target audience).[2] The play *1776* needs no further description to clue the audience; likewise, one of Steven Spielberg's few film bombs, *1941*, needs no further elucidation to intimate clearly that it has something to do with World War II. 1776 is important, especially to Americans, because it is the year in which the United States was born. 1941 is important, again especially to Americans, because with the bombing of Pearl Harbor, the United States formally entered World War II. To those interested in the Middle East, I hope to do something similar to the year 1979 with this book; we know what happened, and the standout individual events themselves have been examined at length, but why is the totality of the 1979 chronology important? Why is it worthy of similar recognition on at least a regional scale? I do not ask "why did *b* happen?"— and answer "because of *a*." I postulate that because *b* happened, *c*, *d*, and *e* happened next.

A distinguishing characteristic of this study may already be perceptible: It will cover a series of important events that occurred throughout the year, whereas other books titled with a "nom de year" typically refer to a specific event within that year that had significant repercussions for the future. Indeed, in modern Middle East historiography, the appellation of most books that deal with the events of 1967 or 1973 in particular is made in direct relation to the Arab-Israeli war that occurred in that year or its many derivatives. For reasons that may ultimately be more coincidence than the result of a linear relationship, the aforementioned seminal events of 1979 were neatly packaged into one year. The Middle East after 1979 would be significantly different from the Middle East prior to 1979. One note is important: This type of temporal examination is avowedly orientalist; that is, I am utilizing a solar calendar year that has been employed in the West (and elsewhere). Since I am examining primarily Middle Eastern events, it would have been entirely appropriate to have employed the Islamic calendar based on the lunar cycle. However, because it is about ten to eleven days shorter than the solar calendar on an annual basis, the aforementioned events would not have all been neatly packaged into one year, thus undermining the raison d'être of this work.[3]

Additionally, the events of 1979 did not *have* to all occur in the same year. As will be discussed later, there *are* some distinct relationships between the various events that did affect each other, some more directly than others; for instance, the taking of the American hostages and most likely the takeover of the Grand Mosque would not have occurred if not for the overthrow of the Shah. But it was not preordained or somehow cosmically controlled that the grand events of that year (the culmination of the Iranian revolution, the Egyptian-Israeli peace treaty, and the Soviet invasion of Afghanistan) would take place within the same calendar year. The Soviets could have easily delayed their invasion by a couple of weeks until January 1980, in which case the central theme of this book would be diluted. It just happened that way. History (and the historians who catalogue it) has a way of presenting periods of specific categorization, and it is often not *entirely* coincidental. But it would probably take an army of astrologers and psychologists to come up with even the semblance of a rationale that would explain why a number of significant events, the commencement of which depended on individual whims and thoughts and unrelated nexuses of historical lines of action, happened to take place within one year.[4] This book will not attempt to offer some defining, overarching theory on why this was the case. It makes more sense to generalize about the propitious environments in which something was more likely to happen than not. Nothing about these events was temporally inevitable. I am more concerned with the changes brought on by this unusual panoply of events.

Most books titled by a year enter directly into a narrative storytelling structure, not unlike a diary of the day-to-day occurrences during a particular period of time seen from the viewpoints of those who were participant observers. These books usually do not offer any serious explanation of the significance of the chosen year or its aftereffects, nor is there any methodological justification given. In James Cameron's *1914*, the author even admits that the book is "a direct narrative, without any especial analysis or philosophy; particularly have I tried to avoid too much hindsight." Cameron goes on to state that his book "is not a work of scholarship, of which there are, fortunately for me, already scores." This is acceptable, I imagine, to those who, as Cameron iterates, want "an impressionist picture of the latter half of a momentous year in the life of a people who, for good or ill, were never to see their world again as they saw it then."[5] It could quite possibly be that the importance of the year 1914 is self-evident, or as Cameron intimates, that the overall significance has been studied ad nauseam, and therefore it needs no further explication. A story from that specific period, drawn from different perspectives, might then be interesting; however, the year 1979 has neither been studied in its totality (chronologically or otherwise) nor been examined as a focal point of change in the Middle East.

Lyn Macdonald's works, *1914* and *1915: The Death of Innocence*, are based essentially on letters, journals, memoirs, and photographs to give voice to those who "might otherwise have gone unheard."[6] The author's task is to "hope that it goes some way toward telling how" things transpired during a block of time without attempting to examine any of the more profound questions associated with this epic event, such as why the war happened when it did ("I would be the last to try to claim that this book comes anywhere near supplying an answer to a question which has exercised the minds of countless historians."), why the book focused on just one year (and why 1914 and 1915 but not 1916, 1917, or 1918), or what the significance was of the year 1914 and/or 1915 in historical terms (or even in terms of the rest of the war).[7] The fact that the second book has a subtitle indicates at least a willingness to offer some explanation of the year's significance, but any hard conclusion or purpose is left up to the reader.

In Virginia Cowles's book, *1913: An End and a Beginning*, the subtitle certainly indicates a break in the usual flow of things, obviously just prior to the outbreak of World War I. But other than a few lines in the opening chapter (there is no preface or introduction to acclimate the reader), there is no historically grounded explanation providing context or meaning for the narrative.[8] There are books on World War I that even focus on a monthly analysis. Immanuel Geiss's edited volume, *July 1914: The Outbreak of the First World War, Selected Documents*, gathers documentary evidence that addresses the vexing question of who was most responsible for the war's outbreak. In this respect, it is similar to those works that examine June 1967.[9] Emil Ludwig's *July '14* expresses itself in prose befitting a dramatic novel or play—it even has "Dramatis Personae of the Great Tragedy."[10] In *November 1918*, Gordon Brook-Shepherd offers a "panorama of the whole closing scene" at the end of the war. In his Forward, Brook-Shepherd begins, almost reluctantly, to make some connections to the global transformation at hand, but ultimately the book is very similar in form to the ones already discussed, offering a narrative of the events leading up to and through the closing act of the war.[11]

As one might expect, World War II also provided the opportunity for some books to be titled with a year. As is the case with those on World War I, these books are essentially in narrative or prose form with little, if any, attempt at historical cause and effect analysis or explanatory models. Richard Collier's *1940: The Avalanche*, contains no preface or introduction, and only on page 270 does the author indicate that the book is "a narrative of 1940"; in addition (and typically), the chapter titles are all in the form of quotes drawn from participant observers.[12] In *1941: Our Lives in a World on the Edge*, William Klingaman spends all of two paragraphs in the epilogue answering the self-directed question, "And in the end, what was the meaning of the year 1941?" Otherwise, it is again a narrative of events as seen through the eyes of contemporaries in a story-telling mode.[13] Klingaman also authored the book *1919: The Year Our World Began*, which obviously refers to the tremendous change in the world, using a measure suitable to our temporally guided lives and history. The books compiled according to this format provide snapshots of a particular time, no more and no less. This is not to diminish their value or utility, but only to point out the differences in tone, style, and intent from this author's work.

Thomas Fleming's *1776: Year of Illusions* is very similar in form and purpose to Klingaman and others mentioned. The world was just a bit different on January 1, 1777, when "William Byrd III arose at dawn and faced the future."[14] Overall, though, it offers scant treatment of the significance of 1776 in terms of connecting direct strands of history from it, however self-evident they may be. This latter point may be the greatest single difference in form and purpose of that book and others like it from this work; that is, the totality of events in the Middle East in 1979 and subsequent change wrought by it is less evident to the uninitiated, therefore obligating more cause and effect extrapolation and analysis. In the field of Middle East history, one book that focuses on one year is Tom Segev's *1949: The First Israelis*, initially published in Hebrew and then translated into English in 1986. It is a revisionist examination of the "first Israelis," that is, those Israeli leaders who established the foundation of the modern state of Israel in the year or so following independence in 1948. In a way, it parallels similar "warts-and-all" historical treatments of America's "founding fathers" that peeled away the layers of reverential myth and legend surrounding them to, at times, reveal less than idealistic individuals who made mistakes and acted incongruously to many of the principles they advocated—although they were not necessarily less heroic. Although the book is an excellent historical excavation, its thrust is purposely narrow, and the ultimate thesis revolves more around building blocks and continuity rather than change. In this way it is similar to Ray Huang's *1587, A Year of No Significance: The Ming Dynasty in Decline*.[15]

Jean Starobinski's *1789: The Emblems of Reason* is an excellent text on the eighteenth century and neoclassicism, divulging the connections between contemporary visual arts and the French Revolution. Its purpose is different from the aforementioned books, as there is a focus on elements of change beyond the politically and militarily observable. Starobinski demonstrates, as other have, that the world (at least Europe) was somehow different as a result of a significant event, in this case the French Revolution. Starobinski also surmises that the English and American revolutions "prevent 1789 from being regarded as an absolute beginning." With any epic event or period there are what seem to be equally important a priori events without which the final sequence in a paradigm would not have occurred.[16] Interestingly, one could also say that the birth of Israel in 1948, the Arab-Israeli wars of 1967 and 1973, or a host of other happenings in the Middle East in the post–World War II era prevent 1979 from being regarded as an "absolute beginning." The independent variable, in its truest form, is well nigh impossible to locate.

Another work that examines change beyond the political realm is James Chandler's outstanding *England in 1819: The Politics of Literary Culture and the Case of Romantic Historicism*.[17] It is a literary history that claims, inter alia, that the roots of the new historicism can be traced back to the Romantic era writings, primarily to the year 1819 (as exhibited in the writings of, inter alios, Shelley, Keats, Byron, Washington Irving). The "Peterloo" massacre at St. Peter's Fields in Manchester, England, on August 16, 1819, when the gendarme killed a number of men, women, and children who were peaceably protesting the state of parliamentary representation, was the political focal point of 1819. The massacre had a variety of cultural repercussions, not the least of which occurred in the literary sphere. It is in this arena where the literary *weltanschauung* emanating out of the Napoleonic era gave way after Waterloo in 1815 to a new historicist literary movement that focused on its self-dated place in time, climaxing in England in 1819.[18] It was, indeed, an "annus mirabilis" that forever changed at least British literary culture.[19]

Chandler's work is one of the few attempts I have found that rigorously examines the methodology of analyzing the events of one calendar year in relation to some overall theme and/or subject. His work is reflective of a certain genre within literary history that, on the whole, has been far more advanced on the subject than those of us in the history discipline.[20]

In discussing the relevant methodological aspects of annualization, Chandler relies heavily on Claude Lévi-Strauss's classic work, *The Savage Mind*, particularly the final chapter on "History and Dialectic."[21] In countering Jean-Paul Sartre's "progressive-regressive" method,[22] Lévi-Strauss insists that "there is no history without dates" and that "dates may not be the whole of history, nor what is most interesting about it, but they are its sine qua non, for history's entire originality and distinctive nature lie in apprehending the relation between *before* and *after*, which would perforce dissolve if its terms could not, at least in principle, be dated" (emphasis the author's).[23]

Lévi-Strauss, however, emphasizes that to the ordinal function of dates must be added a cardinal function, which "indicates chronological distances and densities" of equal duration beyond the simple before and after assignation.[24] Using these various "gauges" of temporal compartmentalization, the "pressure of history" offers up "hot chronologies which are those of periods where in the eyes of the historian numerous events appear as differential elements; others, on the contrary, where for him (although not of course for the men who lived through them) very little or nothing took place."[25] The determination of what is or what is not a "hot chronology" is left up to the individual historian, the compilation of which may or may not be generally agreed upon. After all, the professional historian must have some legitimate license to pick and choose, with consensus and evaluation acting as constraints and approbation. As Robert Gilpin stated, "because history has no starts and stops, one must break into the flow of history at a particular point."[26]

As stated earlier, annualization is but an ordinal class of historical analysis as opposed to the cardinal class of, for example, third, fourth, or sixteenth century. The level of analysis tightens or broadens depending upon whether the historian travels up or down temporal domains that consist of representative classes of dates characterized in hourly, daily, annual, secular (third century, the Romance era, and so on), or millennial terms.[27] The lower the domain (hourly, daily) the more specific the information, and vice versa. For instance, biographical and anecdotal history tends to be in the lower domain mold, or as Lévi-Strauss states, a "low-powered" history that only becomes historically meaningful when juxtaposed and integrated into history of a "higher power than itself."[28]

This Lévi-Straussian categorization is especially relevant to narrative histories and to the choices made by historians of the level of analysis that will guide the extent of historical intrusion and explication. I am less concerned with this aspect of historical analysis than with legitimating and justifying the identification of a "hot chronology" and annualizing it in terms of change and cause and effect relationships. For Lévi-Strauss, the other end of the spectrum consists of "cold" societies that have an internal environment that "neighbors on the zero of historical temperature," resisting "structural modification which would afford history a point of entry into their lives."[29] This supposition of "cold" or "hot" is an evaluative judgment that provides oppositional juxtaposition and, therefore, identification: "But a historical date, taken in itself , would have no meaning, for it has no reference outside itself: if I know nothing about modern history, the date 1643 makes me none the wiser. The code can therefore consist only of classes of dates, where each date has meaning in as much as it stands in complex relations of correlation and opposition with other dates."[30] He goes on to state the following:

> In so far as history aspires to meaning, it is doomed to select regions, periods, groups of men and individuals in these groups and to make them stand out, as discontinuous figures, against a continuity barely good enough to be used as a backdrop. A truly total history would cancel itself out—its product would be nought. What makes history possible is that a sub-set of events is found, for a given period, to have approximately the same significance for a contingent of individuals who have not necessarily experienced the events.[31]

Even if one accepts only part of Lévi-Strauss's "historian's code," based on what might be considered a "hot chronology," the year 1979, in at least one temporal domain and probably even at the higher secular level domain, would meet the criteria of most historians.[32] In view of the fact that the post–World War II era is still recent in terms of historical chronology, we tend to see many more "hot" years than might be identified two hundred years from now. This is especially the case for the Middle East, a region of the globe that has acquired the sobriquet of "hot spot" for most of this period. Even so, the "sub-set" of events in 1979, in my opinion, far outweighs its "colder" annualized neighbors, or at least is "hotter" than the rest within its geographical and temporal classification. 1819 had its Peterloo, but 1979 had its "Peterloo" in the Arab-Israeli arena, in the Gulf arena, in the Central and South Asian arena, and in the abstract arenas of ideology and perception.

Events and Change

Now among the occurrences which must have taken place in the past a vast majority cannot possibly interest the historian. They have never earned a place in accepted history; the historian will never need them for his story. Some occurrences on the other hand appear suitable for insertion in the story, because they possess significance.

—**G. J. Renier,**
History: Its Purpose and Method

It is commonly appreciated that not all happenings within a country from day to day are of "historical" importance. The subject matter of history consists of occurrences which are unusual and out of the common, of events which for one reason or another compel the attention of men, and which are held worthy of being kept in remembrance.

—**Frederick J. Teggart,**
Theory and Processes of History

Webster's Dictionary defines the word "event" as "something that happens: occurrence" and "a noteworthy happening."[33] François Furet defines events as "unique points in time in which something happens that cannot be assimilated to what has come before it or what will come after it. That 'something'—the historical fact promoted to the rank of event—can never be compared, strictly speaking, to a preceding or subsequent fact, since it is its empirically unique nature that determines its importance."[34] Obviously, my contention is that a number of noteworthy happenings occurred in 1979 that caused dramatic change in the Middle East and beyond.

The relationship between events and change has been discussed in a variety of humanities and social science disciplines, primarily in history, political science, and philosophy (it has long been a subject of examination in the physical sciences). The importance of the event as a factor of change has been renewed among historians within the past twenty years or so, particularly in the form of narrative history as a kind of response to the Annales school.[35] Many would say it is in fact the amount of change that determines whether an event of any significance has occurred that could distinguish it from what normalcy essentially is, that is, an ongoing chain of events. All who discuss the subject of change—philosophers, political scientists, historians, and physicists—admit to two types of change: revolutionary versus evolutionary, or dramatic versus slow, substantial versus gradual, or simple change versus transformation. Edgar Morin writes of how one type of event can modify an existing system through disturbances that lead to reorganization, whereas others are essentially confined to being elements within a system that are at once recognizable at certain levels but do not alter the system.[36]

Choosing what is a significant event is a judgment call; some are harder than others to make. Teggart sees events "not as the expression of the will-acts of individuals, but as 'intrusions,' of whatever sort, affecting conditions in which the processes manifested in 'fixity' have been operative without disturbance."[37] He goes on to discuss overall experience, possibly history itself, as being made up of concentric circles, the largest being the universe, the smallest being the individual, with a host of measures in between, ranging from the entire globe to nations to local communities. Accordingly, an event is an intrusion "from any wider circle into any circle or condition which may be the object of present interest."[38] I would submit that an event, certainly a significant event, affects circles not only within the level of transaction but also in outer circles, especially if the delineation of concentric circles is specific to national, regional, and international levels.

The selection process for 1979 is not difficult. Although we must be aware, as Descartes states, that "even the most accurate of histories, if they do not exactly misrepresent or exaggerate the value of things in order to render them more worthy of being read, at least omit in them all the circumstances which are basest and least notable," there are frequently events that are traceable backward and forward as both ends and beginnings.[39] In addition, these events are often surrounded by contemporary pomp and circumstance, which only leaves history to determine whether it was deserved. Indeed, it is the "selection from the available data so arranged as to convey to the reader, not the actual complexity of happenings, but such happenings as the historian considers of importance in a period of time or in a series of occurrences."[40] What might seem significant to one historian might not be to another. However, for the significant events I have identified for 1979, the volume of scholarly examination and populist treatment of each event would suggest otherwise. It seems more likely that the differences of opinion on these events would center on whether each had more positive or negative repercussions over the short and long term.

Each event is also made up of subevents in a time sequence. It is a construction made up of other, smaller constructions. As Peter Munz states:

> The event called the outbreak of World War II can be broken up into innumerable subevents. That does not mean that it did not take place. It only means that it is not hard and fast. It means, further, that some people (in this case, lots and lots of people) decided to place many subevents together in such a way as to give rise to the view that the large event took place. But it is conceivable that other people might have assembled some of the subevents concerned in a different manner and collected others in a different chain.[41]

We all know that World War II is known under different names in the countries that participated in it (as is the case with almost any war); even the beginning and closing dates of the war (as in most wars) are not universally agreed upon. But I am not examining a process, that is, the set of subevents within or that led up to *the* event. At the second that the Ayatollah came to power, the Middle East changed, as history would show; at the second that Menachim Begin and Anwar Sadat signed the Egyptian-Israeli peace treaty with Jimmy Carter presiding, the Middle East changed, as history would show; and at the second that the Soviets invaded Afghanistan, the Middle East changed, as history would show. Ultimately, it was not until Khomeini actually acquired power, until the peace treaty was actually signed, and until Afghanistan was actually invaded that an event worthy of appellation occurred. History would prove these events to be of a higher order. This teleological approach does not attempt to confirm that each of the aforementioned events was significant—this is, by and large, self-evident—but that taken together, occurring within the span of one calendar year, they forever changed the Middle East and, in varying degrees, the international arena as well. Excluding subatomic temporal and historical philosophy, there was in each case a finite moment, an event, that changed things.

There are those who suggest that the concept of the event is "intimately bound up" with the concept of change; one cannot exist without the other.[42] Many say that history is the "science of change," consisting of a chain of an infinite number of events.[43] If this is true, then it stands to reason that significant events cause significant change, especially, as mentioned earlier, if we follow a teleological approach that determines the power of events in terms of the change wrought by them. This anti-Darwinian approach echoes the comments of some of Darwin's critics in terms of nature taking "jumps" from time to time and not always following a methodical evolutionary progression.[44] There are historical events or flash points, so to speak, that move lines of history along at a more accelerated rate and/or in a different direction. The three momentous events of 1979 are certainly flash points, even though they were the culmination of processes at work for many years, if not decades.

Change itself is difficult to pinpoint. There have been attempts at arriving at a formula that defines change, such as the Ancient Criterion of Change and the Cambridge Criterion of Change, both of which assign variables marking time, space, and properties framing a before and after progression during which change clearly occurred.[45] Simple observation dictates that if something is different from that which existed before it was different, then it has changed. But it does not always change completely; there are usually properties of what had existed beforehand even if what is observed connotes total transformation. As Lombard states, "in order for an object to change it must not only survive the change, it must also persist during it, though perhaps not necessarily at every moment."[46] This is not a case of a prince turning into a frog, but a tadpole turning into a frog or a caterpillar into a butterfly.[47] It is a process that reaches a climax or flash point that causes a jump from a to b, in which many of the properties of a still exist in b, but b is markedly different, with unpredictable results to follow.

In 1981, Robert Gilpin's *War and Change in World Politics* was published. In it, he comments upon and analyzes the tremendous change that had occurred throughout the world during the 1970s. He states:

> Political leaders, academic observers, and the celebrated "man in the street" were suddenly conscious of the fact that the energy crisis, dra-

matic events in the Middle East, and tensions in the Communist world were novel developments of a qualitatively different order from those of the preceding decade. These developments and many others in the political, economic, and military realms signaled far-reaching shifts in the international distribution of power, an unleashing of new sociopolitical forces, and the global realignment of diplomatic relations. Above all, these events and developments revealed that the relatively stable international system that the world had known since the end of World War II was entering a period of uncertain political changes.[48]

In 1981 there was a considerable amount of uncertainty, consternation, and instability that painted a foreboding picture of what might lie ahead. Many were equating the situation to that which existed prior to the two world wars, fearing another might be on the horizon, with catastrophic results. A great deal of change had occurred, much of it as a result of events in the Middle East.

Gilpin suggests three types of major international political change that, generally speaking, are "the consequences of the conjuncture of unique and unpredictable sets of developments."[49] These situations result from variations in the distribution of power in the international system, producing disequilibriums in which "economic, political, and technological developments have increased considerably the potential benefits or decreased the potential costs to one or more states of seeking to change the international system."[50] The first type is called systems change, which is a change in the nature of actors within the international system, such as nation-states, empires, or even multinational corporations. The second type is systemic change, in which the governance of an international system or form of control is altered through changes within the system rather than of the system itself. This occurs through the rise or decline of the dominant states or empires that control the system. Interaction change is the third type. Although it is the most prevalent type of change, it is on a relatively lower level than systems or systemic change; it is characterized by modifications in the interactions among actors in the international system, but these modifications do not inherently change the system.[51]

Zeev Maoz defines global change as the "rearrangement of some or all of the units in the system."[52] Whereas Gilpin distinguishes between incremental and revolutionary change, Maoz writes of simple change versus transformation, the latter representing structural change to the system as opposed to nonstructural or nonfundamental changes within the system.[53] We have already seen this demarcation of change under different names, meant to distinguish sudden, dramatic change from evolutionary change. Change takes place all the time, but transformations do not; they are especially worthy of examination because of the implications for global change on varying scales.

Maoz also categorizes three types of approaches to understanding global change: systemic, regional (or subsystemic), and national.[54] The first type, systemic, is kind of a combination of Gilpin's systems change and systemic change, focusing on the result rather than the actual elements that determined the result. In this category, changes take place "due to forces that operate on a global level," such as global war (Gilpin would say hegemonic war), technological breakthroughs, or changes in the decisionmaking of the dominant players in the system. The underlying assumption of this type of change, as Maoz states, is that it is from the top-down, that changes that occur at this global level affect things at lower levels, such as regions and states. This is not unlike Teggart's concentric circles discussed earlier. The second approach is the regional model of change. Here, change occurs in a particular region instead of globally, with repercussions "spilling" over into other regions. In the Middle East, Maoz pinpoints the pan-Arabist (or Arab nationalist) and Islamist movements as examples of ideologies emanating from across a region that "reshape interstate interaction not only within the region but also between regional actors and outside actors." Changes in this model are both top-down and bottom-up; that is, they affect concentric circles above and below the level of interaction.

The third level described by Maoz is the national model of global change, which "rests on a bottom-up causal logic par excellence." In this model, economic, political, and/or social changes within states become a "springboard of global changes." National change, especially that which is revolutionary or transformational, begets regional change, which frequently begets systemic change, particularly when it involves geostrategic and/or political matters. The Iranian revolution is a case in point, where national change certainly affected the region, leading, inter alia, to the Iran-Iraq war, which, as we all know, invited the attention of the global powers, especially since all of this was taking place in an area that contains two-thirds of the world's known oil reserves.

Whereas Gilpin focuses on systems change and systemic change as the roots of global change, admonishing the top-down model that was a convenient fit for the cold war paradigm, Maoz tends to focus on the bottom-up approach delineated in the national model that has become more apparent in the post–cold war environment. Maoz, however, is quick to emphasize that the three models are not mutually exclusive, that there exists a "cycle of change going from one level to another."[55] It is, in fact, a multidimensional matrix that allows for substantial change to be generated in a variety of directions at the same time, with aftereffects that are equally multidirectional. The Middle East in 1979 was one such matrix. As we shall see, change, under any disciplinary definition—historical, philosophical, or scientific—did occur, and it was, by January 1, 1980, of a radical, revolutionary, substantial, dramatic, sudden, and transformational type that affected concentric circles (especially) above and even below the level of activity. Subsequent history would prove it.

Cause and Effect

There are those who suggest that all causes and effects are events and that only events can be causes and effects.[56] It is my assertion that the salient events of 1979 were primary-level causes whose effects were instrumental and widespread; indeed, the mere existence of such important repercussions tends to prove the point. One cannot have a cause without an effect or vice versa, since the effects allow one to trace back and locate the cause(s) and the cause(s) allows one to trace forward to identify various repercussions. Usually historians and social scientists study an event and then go backward in time in order to determine the cause(s). I am essentially traversing in the opposite direction, that is, examining a series of identifiable singular causes/events and extrapolating to future effects/events, which are already history. Certainly the selection of effects narrows the choice of causes, as does the converse, a process that ultimately is quite arbitrary.

Michael Stanford identifies criteria for the selection of a cause (implicitly, that is, a cause worthy of study). Echoing Collingwood, he purports that a cause "is seen as a point of intervention," which is "that factor in the situation which we can most easily control or manipulate."[57] It is also a "variation from the norm," something that is exceptional or unexpected, which is to be distinguished from the necessary conditions that enabled the exceptional event/cause to take place.[58] G. R. Elton distinguishes between "situational causes" that provide the conditions for the "production of a given event" and those causes that directly affect the production of an event.[59] These types of explanations go a long way toward allowing the historian to separate causes of the first order or primary/direct level from other secondary or indirect causes that preceded the event in question, which, in its truest form, is everything that ever happened. And since we cannot trace everything as a linked chain of events (however indirect they may be) all the way back to the Big Bang, it is necessary to have this mechanism in order to narrow the historical field of view.[60] Stanford provides an excellent example:

> In the investigation of a railway accident the inspectors will disregard the speed and load and weight of the train, but pick out the bent rail as the cause of the accident. It is not that the other factors were irrelevant to the crash, but they were present in normal running of the trains. It was the abnormal condition (the bent rail) that they selected as the cause.[61]

Events in 1979 created a (or were *the*) "bent rail," and although some may say that in fact they did lead to a crash, others would agree that they definitely led to changes in direction. As W. H. Walsh comments on the historian's task:

> And what he will want here is to put his finger on the particular point at which things began to go wrong (or for that matter to go right), and to identify the circumstance which, from the point of view of the agent concerned, vitally influenced the outcome. A cause in this sense is a necessary condition of some result, picked out from the remaining conditions

either because it is something which might have been produced or pre-vented at will, or because it was in some way unusual or unexpected.[62]

We must be careful in assessing the engendering elements of the cause(s). In this case, we are focusing on the "What caused what?" and not necessarily on the "Who caused what?"[63] We are examining the occurrence of events and their historical repercussions, which were given appellation (and often different ones by persons from a variety of perspectives) by students and observers of history and politics like myself. They are, within this context, abstract terms that connote well beyond the specific inabstraction from which the terms evolved. Even though this is the case, we must never forget the role of individuals and groups of individuals in the construction of the "what." The choices of individuals, in many cases acting on whims and notions, mold the shape of history, regardless of the structural framework of the environment within which the individual choices were made. This compilation, while not quite Sheldrakian or British antiquarian empiricist, is anything but determinist. As suggested earlier, things could have been quite different, depending upon the largely unpredictable choices made.[64]

When studying cause and effect, one must also be aware of the counter-factual as an element of identification and substantiality. By counter-factual I mean the supposition of what might have happened if the event/cause under discussion had *not* occurred.[65] This type of supposition is based on conjecture at its best (or worst, since ultimately we can only guess at what actually did not happen), but it delineates more clearly the change in direction or "bent rail" that did in fact take place. Without this knowledge, we would be less able to acquire a good sense of what actually did happen and, more importantly, the significance of it. A direct cause under examination can be seen as producing a change of direction in which a number of things occurred within a subset, but it is a different subset than that which would have occurred otherwise. The different subsets produced by the elements of substantial change within a particular geographic and/or political derivation may or may not be intertwined, but history suggests that significant subsets of change are in fact intertwined to at least some degree, or else they would not be significant outside of their own concentric circle. Historical causation is, at its root, a subjective exercise, but the identification process can be one upon which most people agree, leading to a consensus of opinion.

Annales and Narrative

In a previous section within this chapter ("The Examination of One Year"), a number of books titled in an annualized form were delineated, which were, for the most part, in the narrative storytelling mode reflective of what some have called a revival of or return to the narrative form in historical writing in the past twenty or so years.[66] It has been called by some a reaction to the antinarrative "new history" or Annales school of historiography that began in earnest in the 1930s, particularly with the works of Lucien Febvre and Marc Bloch, and that gained the dominant position within the history profession by the 1960s. Not that the narrative form is again attaining the position it held for the more than two thousand years since the time of Homer and Thucydides—far from it. But there has been a noticeable trend in recent years, with some prominent young- and old-school narrative historians (and even some of the self-professed New Historians/Annalistes) leading the way back toward an integration of narration within historical analysis as well as event history through storytelling. In both cases, the importance of the event in historical enunciation, explanation, and causation, a methodology *(histoire événementielle)* held in so much disdain by French structural historians (Annalistes) for decades, has been gaining more and more adherents.[67]

Evolution within the Annales school has made a singular definition difficult, but essentially, the New Historians jettisoned the traditional focus on war, diplomacy, politics, and the elite classes that carried them out and began to utilize interdisciplinary methodologies to examine other facets of society that were at least as important in the movement of history, that is, economic, geographic, demographic, and social factors—facets of society as a whole and not just (or even especially excluding) kings, presidents, and generals. Production of "total history" was the objective not only in terms of longitudinal and latitudinal coverage but also in terms of methodological diversity. As such, political history, which typically encompassed the actions of elite classes, fell into disrepute among Annalistes.[68] In addition, they emphasized history over the long term *(le temps long)* rather than the short term *(le temps court)*, which, de facto, eliminated any examination of singular events or series of events that occurred during a short span of time. In fact, chronological studies, or any sort of temporal categorization, were held in disfavor. The important questions revolved around not when and what happened but why things happened and, influenced by expropriation from anthropological methodologies, what it was like at the time—thematic subject matter associated with rigorous analysis (or what François Furet would call problem-oriented history) rather than mere listings of events.[69] Characteristic of the Annales approach were the frequent appearance of graphs, tables, and other forms of data that measured structural shifts; it was not quite as "bad" as the cliometricians who have enveloped economic history, but it certainly reflected a new focus on measurable factors (what they termed scientific history) that could produce general theories or laws of history (which could be utilized in a predictive fashion as well).[70]

Narrative history, on the other hand, could be called simply a history of events or an account of what happened. Furet, somewhat derisively, calls history the "child of narrative" that "arranges all of its objects of study in a temporal framework: to produce history is to tell a story."[71] Fredric Jameson would say that "the world comes to us in the shape of stories."[72] As Carrard puts it, "the distinguishing feature of narrative is to represent events or situations (more precisely, at least two events or situations) in a time sequence."[73] Certainly the old narrative history focused on war, diplomacy, and politics, or in other words, the great events and figures of history, consigning to oblivion the "nonrelevant" elements of society.

Lately, however, the narrative form of historical writing has incorporated anthropological methodologies to produce the very cultural and social historical snapshots the exclusion of which in the old narrative form the Annalistes were so quick to condemn. This is clearly evident in the works mentioned previously that are titled with the name of a year; these are part of what the French have termed *mentalité,* a mode of narration that details a particular event or short period (or even an individual in biographical format) based on the accounts of eyewitnesses and participant observers. In any event, as Jameson,

Carrard, and others advance, the so-called New Historians were "narrating" and telling stories all along, just in economic, demographic, and mathematic form and not in the fashion of typical political history.[74] Events are not always political, but they can also be economic, demographic, and cultural, and the New Historians "equate narrative with the report of military, political or diplomatic events, whereas other types of occurrence can be arranged in a time sequence and take the form of a story" (Braudel's *La Méditerranée* held out as a case in point).[75] Annaliste studies are never exclusively confined to the synchronic, that is, focused on a specific period of time and all but ignoring historical antecedents, but inevitably delve into the diachronic descriptive mode to at least some degree. As a result of this realization and evolution, Annalistes have been conducting and publishing studies that would have been anathema in the 1950s and 1960s, or as Furet suggests, "the unreasonable ambitions of 'total history' should be lowered."[76] True, behind their narrative-like titles there is a great deal more interdisciplinary analysis and Geertzian detail than is typical in straight narrative history. Although there is an abundance of measured data, there seems to be a synthesis of form, especially among the New Historians, that maintains a level of analytical rigor while broadening the appeal and accessibility of their work. Such has been the metamorphosis within the Annales school that Jean-Pierre V. M. Hérubel, in his bibliographical work on Annales historiography, declared that "no longer is it anathema to write historical accounts of political events or to analyse political phenomena. Certainly Bloch never professed an anti-political history bias. . . . So the trend toward a renewed interest in political events is propelling *Annalistes*."[77] Thus, as Carrard asserts, there has been "an increasing interest in 'short time' after more than two decades of almost exclusive preoccupation with *la longue durée*, a growing concern with the event considered as a factor of change, and a renewed awareness of narrative as a powerful vehicle for making sense of things."[78] Stone comments that the "revival" of narrative is not only due to the undermining of economic and demographic determinism made possible by the importance reattached to ideas, culture, and individual will but also due to a "revived recognition that political and military power, the use of brute force, has very frequently dictated the structure of the society, the distribution of wealth, the agrarian system, and even the culture of the elite."[79] Historiographically, events have again been identified as significant and influential elements of history.

To Jameson, narrative is epistemology, and it thus demands interpretation. Narrative form reveals the manifest, yet knowledge is gained only through discovering the latent meanings of events.[80] Sometimes this "latent meaning" is conveyed by the historian; sometimes it is not. Its determination is left up to the reader. Jameson's recommendation of moving from one form of narrative to another may be closer to the synthesis within the Annales school than the latter would be willing to admit.

As Allan Megill remarks on the process of integration, "cross-disciplinary hybrids, held together by some combination of theory and experience, emerge."[81] Or as Ranke wrote, "history begins with chronicle and ends with essay, that is, in reflection on the historical events that there find special resonance."[82] This present work is a sort of synthesis. It is narrative in its chronological approach and focus on events in terms of cause and effect and delineation of change. Yet it is "annalistic" in its interpretive and interdisciplinary approach, which attempts to uncover the "latent" meaning of the narrative topic under discussion. The appellation of this book invites comparison and elucidation within this framework. It is different, yet at the same time, it is grounded, as all history books are, within previously existing historiographical paradigms. In many ways, it reflects a generation of historians caught in transition. It identifies a watershed in modern Middle East history and attempts to lay the groundwork for an alternative mode of historiography. Historians are indeed a kind of secular priesthood, seemingly endowed with the power and means to select what is and what is not important for the rest of us.[83]

2

The Events

February: The Iranian Revolution

The first major event in the Middle East in 1979 was the culmination of the Iranian revolution, when the Ayatollah Khomeini returned to Teheran on February 1, effectively signaling the end of the reign of Muhammad Reza Pahlavi, otherwise known as the Shah of Iran, and the beginning of the Islamic Republic of Iran. It was, indeed, a momentous occasion, one that would have reverberations the world over, especially in the Persian Gulf region, which contains two-thirds of the world's proven oil reserves (helping, of course, to explain why the revolution's shock waves were felt on a global scale).

As stated in the preface, the aim of this book is not to examine in detail the causes and/or course of the significant events of 1979—this is done at length in a number of other works, the titles of which can be found in the bibliography. At least a trifling of explanation, however, is necessary in order to place these events in their proper context so that a more accurate extrapolation of cause and effect relationships and the nature of the change that took place can be conducted. Even though at the time of these events there was a certain level of agreement as to their momentous character, only history would prove whether this appellation was deserved, a subject to be dissected in the following chapter. The description of the events outlined in this chapter is rudimentary at best and should not be taken as anything more than that.

The causes of any true revolution (and not a coup d'état masquerading as a revolution) are complex and multifarious.[1] Various explanations of the Iranian revolution draw from the historical experience of Iran dating back to the Safavid empire of the sixteenth and seventeenth centuries, the Qajar period in the nineteenth century and Iran's experiences with Russian and British imperialism, and the ravages of World War I, which paved the way for the Pahlavi dynasty to come to power formally in 1925 with the ascension to the peacock throne of Muhammad Reza Shah's father, known to the world as simply Reza Shah. Other explanations focus on the World War II period and its aftermath, when Reza Shah was removed by the British in 1941 because of his perceived pro-German sympathies. His young and untested teenage son was then placed on the throne in 1945, beholden to the British and soon to the Americans, facing a host of challenges that he was ill-equipped to handle alone, particularly one emanating from an austere intellectual liberal constitutionalist named Muhammad Mussadiq, whose overthrow in 1953 was engineered in Washington and London and foreshadowed what would be a widening gulf between the regime and the Iranian people as well as the Shah's increasing dependence on the United States.

Virtually all of the explanations for the Iranian revolution, however, touch at least to some degree on the subject of change resulting from the rapid modernization process the Shah had embarked upon in earnest in the early 1960s. This change had economic, political, and social repercussions, accelerating what Nikki Keddie called the "dual culture" nature of Iranian society, which had, in effect, begun when the Shah's father implemented his own Ataturk-inspired modernization program in the 1920s and 1930s.[2] Whenever there is change of a significant order brought on by regime policy, there are those who benefit from it and there are those who do not. Suffice it to say that the environment for revolutions tends to become much more propitious when the bulk of the population consider themselves in the latter category.

In the 1960s and especially in the 1970s, with the available capital from increased oil revenues resulting from the oil price hike following the 1973 Arab-Israeli war, the Shah embarked upon an economic program that many other countries, particularly in the developing world, also attempted (and with at least equally bad results): import-substituting industrialization or ISI. The idea of ISI was to move nations that were traditionally dependent upon imports for primary and secondary products to an industrial footing. In essence, ISI, riding the crest of the wave of nationalism that had been sweeping across the post–British and French colonial world, was supposed to create economically independent countries that would no longer be subject to the economic, and thus political, whims of the developed world. In Iran, ISI would establish a solid economic foundation for the Shah's dream of making his nation a regional power that also, with the growing dependence of the West upon Middle East oil and at the height of OPEC's influence, would be a player of global significance.

Even though ISI, combined with the Shah's other economic policies based on high oil revenues, resulted in a growing GNP, and thus from the outside Iran seemed to be a Third World success story, internally the economic, political, and social gaps between classes only widened. With ISI's emphasis on heavy industry, the agricultural sector was typically neglected, which directly affected a significant portion of the population since the vast majority of workers were still farmers. Therefore, incomes in the agricultural sector tended to decrease (or at least not increase at nearly as high a rate as bourgeois and upper-class incomes). Small merchants, the bazaaris, also tended to suffer from economic policies designed to the advantage of large-scale manufacturers. In other words, no adequate consumer base was developed that could keep the factories operating at full capacity. As a result, the cost of producing these newly manufactured products built in the ISI-induced factories now located in Iran far outstripped the ability of the vast majority of the population to buy them. The factories, then, with less-than-expected demand, began to operate at less-than-full capacity and less-than-full employment, and economies of scale subsequently drove up the price of the products, which, subsequently, could essentially be purchased only by the upper classes, exacerbating the separation of classes and the frustration felt by those who were not, in their own determination, getting a proper piece of the pie. Because these less-than-efficient factories could not reach the production levels necessary to generate adequate foreign exchange or a tax base that could continue to fuel the process, most developing countries looked to the banks in the United States, Europe, and Japan for loans (and thus began the staggering debt of the 1970s and 1980s that essentially crippled many developing countries). Iran, however, with seemingly unlimited revenues from the sale of oil and natural gas, had the capital to continue this flawed process that from the outside looked promising, but on the inside was causing various sectors of the population to become increasingly disenchanted. It was this disenchantment that the Ayatollah Khomeini and others tapped into and that generated the revolutionary period of 1977–1979.

The Shah also enacted policies and adopted measures of a noneconomic nature that further alienated Iranians from the regime and created more fodder for revolutionary propaganda. Most of this stemmed from an intense megalomania and his obsession with making Iran not only a regional power but a global one. In terms of his domestic policies, the event singled out most often as an indication of the Shah's megalomania and how out of touch he was with the vast majority of his subjects was the $300 million "party" he hosted in 1971 to commemorate the 2500th anniversary of the Achmaenid dynasty, held at the ancient site of Persepolis, one of the capitals of the dynasty during its long tenure in power. Not only was the lavishness and prodigality an affront to many Iranians living in poverty, but the celebration of a pre-Islamic entity or event was offensive to the religious classes (ulama) and to a deeply traditional society as a whole. The Shah's subsequent adoption of the Persian calendar to replace the Islamic calendar reinforced the view that he had an utter disregard and ignorance of the feelings and sensitivities of most Iranians. Beyond the extremely repressive activities that had become a hallmark of the Pahlavi regime, policies such as these only positioned the religious opposition more toward the mainstream of discontent and brought diverse opposition groups closer together.

The Shah's actions in the realm of foreign policy also created a great deal of opprobrium from those sectors of the Iranian population who had already aligned themselves against the Pahlavi regime. First and foremost, the Shah's relationship with the United States, which was largely responsible for maintaining the Shah in power during the Mussadiq crisis in the early 1950s, as well as his related strategic relationship with Israel, fueled the opposition's rallying cries to depose the Iranian monarch. The United States, ironically, had been one of the few external powers for whom most Iranians had positive feelings prior to and immediately after World War II. The fact that the United States did not seem to be interested in the imperialist colonial control that characterized the heyday of European encroachment in the nineteenth century (particularly, in Iran's case, by Russia, Britain, and France), cast Washington in a favorable light. Combined with the idealism of Wilsonian self-determination proclaimed during World War I and the self-described morally based foreign policy that set it apart from Europe, the United States was, in fact, considered a friendly balancing act to continuing British and Russian pressure. The presence of American economic and military advisors became more pronounced after World War I, and Washington's influence in Teheran proportionately increased after World War II with the postwar contraction of British influence.

With the onset of the cold war with the Soviet Union following World War II, however, Iran's strategic significance in terms of geography (with long borders with the U.S.S.R. and on the Persian Gulf) and geology (oil and natural gas) soared from the vantage point of Washington. As such, preventing the expansion of Soviet influence in the Persian Gulf and preserving stability in the Gulf region (in order to maintain the steady flow of oil from the Gulf at reasonable prices) became the two hallmarks of U.S. foreign policy in the area.

The election in Iran of Muhammad Mussadiq as prime minister in 1951, ostensibly because of his popular stance against the economic usurpation of the Anglo-Iranian Oil Company (AIOC, later British Petroleum) as well as his call for a more independent and neutralist foreign policy, sounded a clear warning bell in London and Washington. Despite the fact that he was an avowed liberal constitutionalist, who on the surface should have appealed to the United States, the Truman and (particularly) Eisenhower administrations saw him as a potential threat, primarily because of his willingness to associate his National Front party with the communist Tudeh party traditionally supported by the Soviet Union. London and Washington schemed, therefore, to remove Mussadiq from power and secure the Shah's hold on the throne. In the infamous operation engineered by the CIA in 1953, this is exactly what happened, in the process of which the young Shah became ever more paranoid and dependent on the United States. The people in general, however, were tremendously disillusioned by Washington's actions, and the United States, in their eyes, now joined the unenviable ranks of the imperialist powers. The vicious cycle of the relationship between the Shah and successive American administrations grew to the point where by the early 1970s opposition to the Shah was the same as opposition to the United States—the vehemence attached to one was equaled by the vehemence attached to the other.

The strategic nature of the Iranian-U.S. relationship grew by leaps and bounds with the promulgation of the Vietnam-induced Nixon Doctrine of 1969, which, in essence, called on America's allies to shoulder more of the burden of defense against communist aggression worldwide while the United States was bogged down in Southeast Asia and suffering from the Vietnam War's deleterious economic repercussions. In the Middle East, this meant more support for Iran to act as Washington's gendarme in the Gulf arena as well as more support for Israel in the Arab-Israeli arena, which after the 1970 Jordanian crisis also proved itself to be a worthy recipient of almost limitless U.S. military aid in order to curtail Soviet influence and that of its allies. This convergence of interests naturally produced close Iranian-Israeli strategic ties, especially since both shared a common enemy, Iraq.

The Shah proved that he was at least somewhat worthy of U.S. military support when Iran successfully helped the Sultanate of Oman put down its Marxist-supported (through the Popular Front for the Liberation of the Arab Gulf or PFLOAG) Dhofari revolt. Probably no other foreign official has had such direct and almost limitless access to conventional U.S. military assistance. As someone stated at the time, it was like giving the keys to the biggest liquor cabinet in the world to a confirmed alcoholic. So many more weapons were purchased than was necessary that in one particular year in the 1970s there was a shortage of cement for housing foundations because most of it was being used to build bunkers for all of the new military hardware. The oil price hike following the 1973 Arab-Israeli war only provided the Shah with more wherewithal to match his megalomaniac ambitions.

Of course, all of this was not lost on most Iranians. Not only was American economic and military imperialism rearing its ugly head from the point of view of many in Iran, but Western cultural imperialism also was seen as a serious threat to Iran's Islamic heritage and tradition. The Shah's party at Persepolis, his continuing neglect of the populace, and his domestic prodigality and spendthrift foreign and defense policies only exacerbated the growing gulf between the regime and its elite-class support base and the remainder of the Iranian people. The Shah was seen as doing the bidding of the United States and Israel, and both Washington and Tel Aviv were viewed as instruments directing the Shah's policies of repression and neglect. One only has to scan the speeches of the Ayatollah Khomeini before and during the revolutionary period to understand how effectively he tied the Shah to the United States and Israel as the focal points of the opposition.[3]

In most revolutionary environments, there needs to occur an event or a series of events, what I term flash points, that coalesce elements of the opposition and fuel the revolutionary fervor that bridges the oftentimes large gap between a vocal opposition and actually taking the actions necessary to overthrow the regime. These flash points also often bring to the fore various groups or individuals who seize the moment and rise to leadership positions within the movement. This was certainly the case in Iran during the revolutionary period of 1977–1979.

First, there was the death of Khomeini's son, Mustafa, in Iraq in October 1977, which was assumed by the Ayatollah and his followers to be the work of SAVAK, the Shah's security apparatus. Then, in January 1978, a government-sanctioned article appeared in a semi-official newspaper attacking Khomeini, who, though not the most popular or powerful of the ayatollahs in Iran, had substantial and vociferous backing among many of the bazaaris, students, poor city-dwellers, and peasants. Protests to the article broke out the next day in the religious city of Qum, resulting in a riot that left more than seventy protesters killed. Many view this episode as the turning point in the revolution, when the initiative of the protest movement shifted from the secular forces to the religious opposition, especially its radical element led by Khomeini. Finally, in September 1978, an apparent misunderstanding about the timing of a curfew announcement following a peaceful march of more than one million people in Teheran led to the deaths of up to one thousand Iranians killed in a follow-up demonstration. This tragic event, known in Iran as Black Friday, essentially ended any hope of accommodation between most elements of the opposition and the regime. It is also when many Iranians began to see the value of

Khomeini's uncompromising stand, which he had been enunciating for years; the Shah had to go and an Islamic republic had to be formed.

More moderate alternative solutions, such as the constitutional monarchy advocated by elements of the reconstituted National Front, had very little chance of succeeding because of the virulent anti-Shah hostility, which was vividly displayed in huge demonstrations and widespread strikes. By the time the Shah appointed Shahpour Bakhtiar prime minister in December 1978, someone who had been a vocal critic of the Shah as a member of the National Front, it was too little, too late. The Shah effectively abdicated by leaving the country on January 16, 1979, weak from the cancer that would take his life shortly thereafter and despondent over how everything had gone so wrong so quickly. All that was left was for Khomeini to triumphantly return on February 1, forcing the Bakhtiar government to dismember itself within a few days, and begin the task of consolidating power and changing Middle East history.

March: The Egyptian-Israeli Peace Treaty

When Israeli Prime Minister Menachem Begin and Egyptian President Anwar Sadat met at the White House on March 26, 1979, and signed the Egyptian-Israeli peace treaty with President Jimmy Carter presiding over the ceremony and witnessing the agreement, most everyone knew the Middle East had changed in a profound manner. What people did not know with complete certainty was the direction of that change and whether it would be for better or worse. Everyone seemed to have an opinion, the intensity of which increased as the consequences of the peace treaty became clear.

To understand the origins of the treaty, one has to begin with the decisive Israeli military victory during the June 1967 Arab-Israeli war. As is well known, during this six-day conflict, Israel acquired the Golan Heights from Syria, the West Bank from Jordan, and the Gaza Strip and the Sinai Peninsula from Egypt. Israel suddenly had the strategic depth it had been lacking since its creation in 1948. It also had many more Palestinians under occupation, a situation that would prove to be more and more politically unpalatable as time passed. In essence, a bargaining situation had been established, with the prospect of Israel trading back the lands it had occupied during the war in return for peace, secure borders, and normalization of relations with its Arab neighbors. This land-for-peace formula was crystallized in the now-famous United Nations Security Council Resolution 242 passed in November 1967 in response to the new Arab-Israeli circumstances. Despite its ambiguities, it is a formula that to this day remains the basis for Arab-Israeli negotiations.

The problem with this new bargaining situation was that it was asymmetrical; that is, Israel held all of the land. The Arabs, after being so thoroughly defeated and humiliated in six days by the Israelis, were not about to engage in negotiations from a position of weakness. Before negotiations could occur, the Arabs needed to improve their bargaining position and shatter the aura of invincibility that seemed to pervade Israel following the war. Indeed, contrary to what most thought would be the appropriate postwar policy, Egypt's President Gamal Abd al-Nasser, long the standard-bearer of the Arab nationalist movement, pursued again the war option with Israel instead of peace negotiations by initiating what came to be known as the War of Attrition in 1969–1970, the object of which was to fight an incremental and drawn-out war that worked to the advantage of Egypt because of its greater numbers of troops and materiel rather than a short, mobile war that was to Israel's advantage. The general goal of the War of Attrition was to improve the Arab strategic and bargaining position vis-à-vis Israel.

Ironically, the War of Attrition, which led directly to the Jordanian civil war in September 1970, known in Palestinian circles as Black September, resulted in quite the opposite situation.[4] It was Israel's timely warnings and movement of troops that deterred further Syrian involvement against Jordanian forces in their attempt to drive out the Palestine Liberation Organization, which by then had become something of a state within a state, with Amman acting as its headquarters. This indicated to the Nixon administration, in particular, National Security Adviser Henry Kissinger, that Israel could be a valuable cold war asset in preventing the expansion of Soviet influence in the Middle East (in this case, through Syria). This new Israeli role was consistent with the Nixon Doctrine, and as a result, the United States began to provide enormous amounts of military aid to Tel Aviv, similar to what Washington was doing with Iran. This only stiffened Israeli resolve to hold onto the occupied territories, or at least force the Arab states to come to the bargaining table on Israeli terms, since it seemed obvious that the Arabs could not militarily defeat Israel or even through military pressure improve their strategic position. A stalemate on the Arab-Israeli front thus ensued, which was the situation that Anwar Sadat inherited when he became president of Egypt soon after Nasser's death in 1970 during attempts to mediate the Jordanian situation.

Sadat knew that the legitimacy of his regime rested on his ability to return the Sinai Peninsula to Egyptian control, either through peace or war. Not only was there the political and psychological necessity to reacquire the Sinai, but there were also a number of practical reasons. Three of the four pillars of the Egyptian economy in terms of generating foreign exchange were directly or indirectly related to the level of tension on the Arab-Israeli issue. First, since most of the oil reserves in Egypt were located in or astride the Sinai Peninsula, this revenue-producing activity was obviously in abeyance while Israel held the territory. Second, Egypt relies heavily on Suez Canal tolls, but the canal had been blocked since 1967, and in any event, Israel held the east bank of the Suez Canal in the Sinai and could easily impede passing ships. Third, because of its unique pharaonic and Islamic history, Egypt counts on tourism to generate revenues and foreign exchange; however, tourism declined sharply after the 1967 war and the War of Attrition, and it remained depressed when Arab-Israeli tensions were high, which was certainly the case in the early 1970s.[5] In addition, if a settlement could be achieved with Israel, Egypt could redirect a significant portion of its defense expenditures toward more productive purposes—augmented by tremendous amounts of U.S. military and economic assistance. (Egypt has, in fact, become the second largest recipient of U.S. foreign aid, after Israel.) For these economic reasons, Sadat felt compelled to focus the entirety of his efforts on regaining the Sinai.

Sadat, at first, attempted to regain the Sinai through diplomatic measures by indicating his willingness to accept a negotiated solution. In one case, direct United Nations mediation through its special emissary, Gunnar Jarring, led to the Jarring plan, which Sadat accepted and

Israel rejected. With an increasingly stalemated diplomatic situation by 1972, Sadat felt the need for a breakthrough. As history would show, Sadat had a propensity for dramatic and bold moves, and in July 1972 he expelled about 15,000–20,000 Soviet advisors. There was certainly an internal rationale for this act, such as appeasing his own military by getting rid of the heavy-handed Russian military advisors and/or making an initiation of hostilities with Israel a more viable option by eliminating the possibility of Moscow tipping off the United States or pressuring Cairo to stand down. But Sadat saw this as primarily an overture to Washington in order to activate the diplomatic process and break the stalemate.

The only problem with Sadat's calls for a negotiated settlement was that the United States and Israel were essentially not listening, and his actions went virtually unnoticed in Washington and Tel Aviv. The reason for this seemingly negligent posture on the part of the United States relates directly to the events that transpired during the Jordanian civil war in 1970. The civil war emerged as a contest for power between the Jordanian monarch, King Hussein, and the Palestine Liberation Organization (PLO), which had located its headquarters in Amman and had for all intents and purposes become a state within a state. Since the majority of the population in Jordan consisted of Palestinians, that is, those Arabs who had lived in pre-1948 Palestine or in the West Bank occupied by Israel in the 1967 war and had migrated to Jordan as refugees, this was a very serious threat to the survival of the Hashemite monarchy, a regime that traditionally had good relations with the United States and an unspoken working relationship with Israel. In other words, this was a regime that both Washington and Tel Aviv wanted to remain in power. However, it was also a regime that certain Arab countries, in particular, Syria, would not mind seeing overthrown, since Hussein was perceived as being too moderate in his position vis-à-vis Israel and too beholden to the United States. As such, the radical Ba'thist regime in Syria, which essentially had initiated the events that led to the 1967 war, again took bold steps to improve its position in the inter-Arab arena by sending forces into Jordan in support of the PLO. The Nixon administration sent the Sixth Fleet to the eastern Mediterranean in an attempt to intimidate Syria, but since Damascus was ostensibly protected by its patron the Soviet Union, it could, and did, call the American bluff. Nixon did not want this episode to spiral into a superpower confrontation, especially not when U.S. forces were bogged down in Vietnam and Cambodia.

An alternative appeared in the form of an Israeli deterrent. Israeli forces massed on the Syrian border, threatening to intervene if Syria did not cease and desist its support of the PLO in Jordan. Syrian forces paused and eventually retreated, particularly after the then acting defense minister and commander of the air force, Hafiz al-'Asad, ever the pragmatic strategist, refused to commit the Syrian air force to the Jordanian theater.[6] King Hussein's troops, now operating under what was in effect an Israeli defensive umbrella, could with more fortitude and aggressiveness move against the PLO, resulting in the successful expulsion of the PLO out of Jordan.[7]

The utility of Israel was not lost among policymakers in Washington, particularly National Security Adviser Henry Kissinger, with his brand of realpolitik and cold war zero-sum foreign policy. It was clear from this episode that Israel could be a valuable cold war ally against Soviet expansionism, especially that which might occur through its own client states in the region, such as Syria. Greater reliance on regional allies was also consistent with the Nixon Doctrine promulgated in 1969, which essentially called on U.S. allies to shoulder more of the burden of the cold war. Although initially aimed at the situation in Southeast Asia, the doctrine came to be applied to the Middle East, where Iran under the Shah would be the U.S. gendarme of the Persian Gulf, and Israel would be Washington's bulwark against Soviet influence in the heartland of the Arab world. As such, American military and economic aid to Israel exploded, making Israel seem even more invincible than it was following the 1967 Arab-Israeli war.

Diplomatically, this new strategic partnership translated into a rigid position on negotiations concerning the occupied territories and UN Resolution 242. Because of Israel's military dominance, the Arab states would have to come to the bargaining table on terms that were closer to the Israeli optimum bargaining position; in other words, the idea that the Arab states, individually or in combination, would militarily confront a victorious Israel that was now enthusiastically backed by the United States was barely entertained. The Arabs would be forced to negotiate through Washington if they hoped to regain Israeli occupied territory, a process that would exclude the Soviet Union. In this light, then, Sadat's expulsion of the Soviet advisers, rather than signaling a clear message that Egypt was ready and willing to reactivate diplomacy, was seen in Washington as a sign that its stand-firm policy was working—that Egypt was moving away from the Soviets and that the policy should therefore continue unabated. In addition, détente between the Soviets and the Americans was the primary foreign policy consideration at this stage in both Moscow and Washington, including mutual pledges not to take advantage of the other superpower's problems and predicaments in the Third World. Although the Nixon administration clearly had Vietnam in mind, it did not want to be seen as breaking these pledges in Egypt so soon after they were exchanged during a summer 1972 summit meeting between President Nixon and Soviet Premier Leonid Brezhnev. The bottom line was that the diplomatic stalemate on the Arab-Israeli front continued, and Sadat felt something had to be done in order to break it.

If diplomacy could not be reactivated and the stalemate could not be broken by kicking out Russians, pursuing UN peace missions, or appealing to Washington, then maybe it could be accomplished through war. And this is exactly what Sadat did. He utilized the Cairo-Damascus-Riyadh axis to launch a simultaneous surprise invasion of Israel. Egypt attacked across the Suez in the south, and Syria moved through the Golan Heights in the north, all of which was backed up by Saudi influence in the Organization of Petroleum Exporting Countries (OPEC) to unleash, if necessary, the oil weapon—an oil embargo that would force the United States to intervene either to save the Arabs from total destruction if things turned for the worse or to enter the fray as an active mediator ready to pressure Israel to make the necessary concessions for peace (or both).[8]

The Israelis were caught off guard by the attack primarily because they were convinced that the Arabs would not initiate an all-out war unless they knew they could win. However, Sadat did not launch the 1973 Arab-Israeli war on October 6 to defeat Israel or even to regain the territory lost in the previous war; he did it to achieve the more limited objectives of reactivating diplomacy and improving, if possible, Egypt's bargaining position with Israel by at least establishing a bridgehead on the east bank of the Suez Canal.[9] This the Egyptians accomplished.

Although by the end of the war the Israelis were on the verge of routing the Egyptians and Syrians, the Arab combatants had shown that Israel could be bloodied, and Egypt did maintain its hold of the east bank of the Suez Canal in the Sinai. In addition, with the unleashing of the oil weapon during the war and the subsequent quadruple increase in the price per barrel of oil by early 1974, the Arabs now had newfound bargaining power.

The more symmetrical bargaining situation created by the war was seized upon by Henry Kissinger. By manipulating to a certain extent the outcome, he was able to position the United States as the primary broker of the postwar negotiations while keeping the Soviets on the sidelines and drawing the Egyptians closer to Washington.[10] The tireless shuttle diplomacy, which resulted in the disengagement agreement between Israel and Egypt in January 1974 (otherwise known as Sinai I), was, in effect, the first step toward the Egyptian-Israeli peace treaty of 1979.[11]

Succeeding President Nixon after his resignation in August 1974, President Gerald Ford, with Secretary of State Henry Kissinger leading the way, viewed the disengagement agreements following the 1973 war as a stepping-stone toward convening an international conference in Geneva that would generate a comprehensive Arab-Israeli peace. For a variety of reasons, however, an international peace conference, much less a comprehensive peace accord, was not feasible at this time. The many obstacles included the nature of Palestinian representation (after the 1974 Arab League summit meeting in Rabat, Morocco, the PLO was declared the sole legitimate representative of the Palestinian people, but Israel officially viewed it as a terrorist organization and refused to negotiate with the PLO), differences among the Arab states in trying to formulate a unified position, disagreement about what role, if any, the Soviets would play, and traditional Israeli opposition to any international peace conference that would increase the pressure for Israeli concessions.

As a result of this impasse, the United States, Israel, and Egypt agreed that another limited disengagement agreement similar to Sinai I was in order—in essence, another step. Even this was terribly diffi-

cult to achieve, and only after some very tough negotiating on the part
of Kissinger, Sadat, and Israeli Prime Minister Yitzhak Rabin, as well
as a temporary rift in U.S.-Israeli relations in the summer of 1975, was
anything accomplished. The result was another Egyptian-Israeli disengagement agreement, otherwise known as Sinai II, in which it was
agreed that Israeli forces in the Sinai would pull back beyond the
strategically important Giddi and Mitla passes in return for the establishment of a more formal demilitarized buffer between Egypt and
Israel; these moves would be supervised by the United Nations and
monitored by American-controlled and manned sophisticated elec-
tronic early warning stations. Egypt also agreed to several clauses com-
mitting itself to non-belligerency, a peaceful resolution of the Arab-
Israeli conflict, and efforts to draw other Arab states, particularly
Syria, into similar agreements.

The fact that Syria did not follow Egypt's lead at this time clearly
indicated that Sadat was willing to stake out his own path apart from
the rest of the Arab world despite the continued façade of commitment to the Palestinian issue. He did not want to seem to be alone
among the Arab states negotiating with Israel. In order to facilitate the
deal, the Ford administration increased U.S. military and economic aid
to Israel and promised to assist Egypt in its economic development,
which included an opening-up of the economy *(infitah)* to foreign
investment and the private sector. Kissinger also agreed to an Israeli
demand that the United States not recognize or negotiate with the
PLO until the PLO recognized Israel, accepted UN Security Council
resolutions 242 and 338, and renounced terrorism. This demand,
which seemed innocuous at the time, was agreed to in order to get the
Israelis to sign on to Sinai II, but it eventually hampered Washington's
attempts to position itself as an honest broker in the Arab-Israeli
arena. However, Kissinger felt the alternative was war, which could
result in enhanced Soviet influence and possibly another oil embargo.
In addition, it was feared that a regional war could spiral out of control
into another U.S.-Soviet confrontation. U.S. foreign policy in the
Middle East rested on continuing to pull Egypt into its orbit and supporting Sadat's pursuit of a peaceful resolution of the Arab-Israeli conflict, with the hope that it would draw in other moderate Arab states
such as Saudi Arabia and Jordan.

Sinai II was immediately criticized and condemned by a number of groups in the United States. The thinking went as follows: If so much energy was expended, so many promises made, and so much aid given just to get the Israelis to withdraw some 30 kilometers in the Sinai, what in the world would it take to bring about a comprehensive peace accord that included Israeli withdrawal to its pre-1967 Arab-Israeli war borders? In addition, Kissinger's approach seemed only to be averting war by buying time rather than achieving comprehensive peace by addressing the problems at the root of the conflict. Indeed, a Brookings Institution report issued in late 1975 concluded that the step-by-step approach had exhausted itself, leaving too many issues unresolved, which could lead to rising tensions and, subsequently, all-out war in the region that could escalate into a superpower confrontation similar to that which occurred during the latter stages of the 1973 Arab-Israeli war.[12] Besides, as Sinai II so vividly displayed, the price paid for these limited agreements became too prohibitive. The time had come for a comprehensive settlement.

Jimmy Carter became president after winning the 1976 election, and he came into office with the Middle East as a high priority within his foreign policy platform. Basing his approach to a significant degree upon the 1975 Brookings Institution report, Carter sought at first to convene an international conference in Geneva, Switzerland, with the expressed purpose of seeking a comprehensive settlement in order to avert a superpower standoff. Unfortunately for the Carter administration, many of the same issues that prevented the convening of a conference under the Ford administration still existed, with the added divisiveness and preoccupation created in the Arab world due to the outbreak of the Lebanese civil war in 1975–1976. In addition, a window of opportunity may have been lost when, in May 1977, Menachem Begin became prime minister of Israel, leading the right-wing Likud party to power for the first time in Israeli history. The Likud party had adopted a hard-line approach toward negotiations with the Arab states and was much more reluctant to return land for peace than their Labor party counterparts, wanting to keep most, if not all, of the occupied territories for strategic and/or religious reasons. Begin also greatly accelerated the Jewish settlement process in the occupied territories in order to establish facts on the ground, thus making it that much more difficult for any future Israeli government, whether Likud or Labor, to trade land for peace.

As a result, a stalemate ensued in the Arab-Israeli prospective peace process. As he had done in 1973 during another diplomatic lull, Anwar Sadat in 1977 engineered another bold move in order to break the stalemate. In 1973 Sadat chose war; in November 1977 he made the incredibly dramatic gesture of visiting Israel, the first official visit by any Arab head of state. With his visit and speech before the Israeli Knesset or parliament, Sadat implicitly recognized Israel, again, the first Arab head of state to do so, convinced skeptical Israelis that Egypt was serious about peace, and perforce restored momentum to the peace process. Sadat, and many other Egyptians as well, felt that Egypt had spilt enough blood, indeed much more than its share, in confronting Israel. Now the time had come to give primary consideration to Egyptian national interests, especially in terms of what an agreement with Israel that returned the Sinai could do for Egypt's ailing economy. The Egyptian president had grown impatient with a process that never seemed to get going—it needed a kick-start. Instead of dealing with Israel en masse, Egypt would show the way, expecting that a separate deal would compel countries such as Jordan, Saudi Arabia, and possibly even Syria to do the same, knowing full well that they could no longer confront Israel without Egypt.

Sadat's historic visit did not elicit the forthcoming response from Begin that was hoped by the Egyptian regime. The Israeli prime minister's own militant background, as well as his support base within Israel that wanted to hold on to the occupied territories for strategic and/or religious reasons, created a reluctance to engage in a process that portended expansion from Egyptian-Israeli bilateral issues toward an overall discussion of the Palestinian problem. Begin did not close the door completely, however, for he saw this as a possibly unique opportunity to engage in direct, one-on-one negotiations, the type Israelis had traditionally preferred since it gave them more leverage over each individual Arab state and prevented, as mentioned previously, a coalition of forces gathered at an international peace conference from pressuring Israel to make concessions it did not want to make or imposing a solution from the outside. In addition, separating Egypt from the rest of the Arab world had been a long-standing Israeli goal as a way to weaken Arab bargaining power and remove the greatest single military threat to Israel, which, for many in the Likud party especially, would make it easier to hold onto the rest of the occupied territories (after presumably returning the Sinai Peninsula to Egypt) and to downgrade, if not totally ignore, the Palestinian situation.[13] In other words, while the United States and Egypt saw a possible Egyptian-Israeli peace agreement as a stepping-stone toward a comprehensive Arab-Israeli peace that resolved the Palestinian problem, Begin and his cohorts saw it as the endgame, which, in their view, adequately met the UN Security Council Resolution 242's ambiguous call for a "withdrawal of Israeli armed forces from territories (and not *the* territories) occupied" in the 1967 June war (parenthetical insert mine). This would also buy time for Israel to build more settlements in the remaining occupied territories.

By the summer of 1978, it was clear that any hope for an Egyptian-Israeli peace agreement needed outside intervention to break the many impasses that had developed between Begin and Sadat.[14] President Carter, not wanting to see the process totally derailed, which might undermine Sadat's position in Egypt with untold consequences, inserted himself directly into the fray by inviting both Begin and Sadat to the presidential retreat at Camp David in September 1978 to hash out a framework for peace.

For thirteen tumultuous and dramatic days, the participants bargained extremely hard in order to at least come away with something from the effort. The talks came to the precipice of breaking down on numerous occasions; indeed, after initial meetings between the three leaders, Begin and Sadat did not meet face to face for the remainder of the Camp David talks, with President Carter carrying out his own bit of shuttle diplomacy from one cabin to another.

With Begin having less to lose from a failure to reach agreement, perforce Sadat was the one who made most of the concessions, usually with pressure from Carter, since he knew that Begin would be harder to budge. Ultimately, the final result became known as the Camp David accords, which consisted of two frameworks for peace. One was titled "A Framework for the Conclusion of a Peace Treaty between Egypt and Israel," which dealt with bilateral Egyptian-Israeli issues, including a phased Israeli withdrawal from the remainder of the Sinai

Peninsula in return for the establishment of full normal diplomatic, economic, and cultural relations between the two countries. The second framework was titled "A Framework for Peace in the Middle East," which was intended to provide for a comprehensive settlement to the Arab-Israeli problem based on UN Security Council Resolution 242 in all its parts, including a resolution to the Palestinian problem.

After several more months of haggling on all sides, including shuttle diplomacy by Carter in the Middle East, the Egyptian-Israeli peace treaty, the first between Israel and an Arab state, was signed in Washington with President Carter presiding on March 26, 1979. The treaty essentially reflected the Camp David accords, consisting of the two frameworks for peace negotiated at the presidential retreat, which, as the treaty's critics quickly pointed out, were not indelibly linked with each other; that is, progress on the one track, the Egyptian-Israeli bilateral agreement, would not necessarily have to be matched by progress on the other track, a comprehensive Arab-Israeli settlement dealing with the Palestinian issue. Nevertheless, for better or worse, the Middle East would never be the same.

December: The Soviet Invasion of Afghanistan

It was geographically fated that the history of Afghanistan, a country bordering the southern underbelly of Czarist Russia and then the Soviet Union, would be indelibly linked with its large neighbor to the north. Throughout much of the nineteenth century, Afghanistan was a pawn in the "great game" being played out between Great Britain and Czarist Russia, largely over British concerns about protecting its prized imperial possession, India, against Russian encroachment due to the latter's perpetual objective of gaining year-round access to warm-water ports. This British-Russian rivalry was finally resolved with the 1907 Anglo-Russian Convention in which Moscow declared that Afghanistan was formally outside of its sphere of influence and agreed to conduct relations with the Afghans through the British; in return, London agreed not to occupy or annex Afghanistan.

The Bolshevik Revolution in 1917, creating the Soviet Union, reignited the tensions between London and Moscow and again heightened the strategic importance of Afghanistan. Increasingly feeling under siege from the anticommunist West in the period immediately following World War I, Moscow began to see Afghanistan as an important defensive buffer against Western, particularly British, encroachment. In addition, the new Soviet regime, inspired by its new revolutionary doctrine, determined that Afghanistan could also be a strategic launching point to foment instability for the British in its South Asian possessions. As Leon Trotsky once noted, "the road to Paris and London lies through the towns of Afghanistan, the Punjab, and Bengal."[15] December 1979 was not the first time in the twentieth century that the Soviet Union had militarily intervened in Afghanistan. Consistent with its strategic and ideological interests, the Soviet Union had crossed the border of its southern neighbor on at least three prior occasions: 1925, 1929, and 1930. Although none of these were on the scale of the 1979 invasion (they were more on the level of limited incursions to chase down bandits seeking refuge), they do indicate the long-held Soviet interest in Afghani affairs since the post–World War I period and the desire to ensure the favorable disposition of a succession of Afghani regimes toward Moscow.

Afghanistan is a country that was essentially formed by default, that is, whatever was left between the borders of its neighbors. It is an ethnically diverse country, with Pushtuns, Tajiks, and Uzbeks accounting for the three largest groups. This heterogeneity, compounded by the mountainous geography of Afghanistan, has engendered little or no national consciousness and has made it extremely difficult for any Afghani regime to actually control the country in anything more than a loose confederation of the plethora of powerful tribes throughout the land. As Thomas Hammond points out, when someone in Afghanistan is asked, "What are you?" most, especially those residing outside of the major cities, will respond by identifying themselves as Pushtun, Uzbek, or Tajik rather than Afghani.[16]

Indeed, it could be said that as long as the ruling regime was bland and somewhat indifferent, Afghanistan could exist in relative stability. Whenever the regime attempted to assert itself by instituting far-reaching reforms, it invariably encountered severe resistance from the tribal-dominated countryside, which basically wanted to see the maintenance of the status quo and government authority confined to the cities. This accounts for the long reign of King Muhammad Zahir from

1933 to 1973. He was a rather weak and ineffectual monarch, but he also did not get in anybody's way or stir up trouble with the powerful tribal leaders. This would change in 1973, when a member of the royal family, Prince Muhammad Daoud, ousted King Zahir from power and declared an end to monarchy and the beginning of the Republic of Afghanistan. The environment that brought about the occasion of the Soviet invasion in 1979 can be traced back to this event.

Daoud had been the strongman under King Zahir as prime minister during much of the 1950s and early 1960s until he was forced out in 1963, probably because he was becoming too powerful within the government. Daoud was a natural choice for the coup plotters in the military since he had been the one primarily responsible for building up a close strategic relationship with the Soviet Union, which benefited the Afghan armed forces over the years.[17] He was also initially supported by leftist parties, with considerable conjecture that the Soviet Union, at least to some degree, helped engineer the coup.[18] With the proclamation of the republic, Daoud assumed the titles of both president and prime minister and was now in a position to implement political, social, and economic reforms that, in his view, would lift Afghanistan out of its isolated and impoverished condition.

Daoud turned out to be a bit more independent than the Soviets would have liked. Soon after coming to power, he reduced the power of leftist groups, particularly the People's Democratic Party of Afghanistan (PDPA). The PDPA had been formed in 1965, but it split in 1967 into two groups, Khalq ("masses") and Parcham ("banner"). Khalq was led by Nur Muhammad Taraki and Hafizullah Amin, while Parcham was led by Babrak Karmal. All three men would figure prominently in the events leading up to and through the Soviet invasion in 1979. The division between Parcham and Khalq was, in part, ideologically and ethnically based (Khalq was dominated by Pushtuns, whereas Parcham tended to be non-Pushtun), but the personal animosity between Taraki and Babrak is what really drove the separation. Both factions enjoyed good relations with the Soviet Union and were supported by Moscow, thus Daoud's actions against both equally concerned the Kremlin.

Daoud also improved Afghanistan's relations with its pro-U.S. neighbors, Iran and Pakistan. In fact, in 1974 the Shah of Iran, no doubt with U.S. approval, promised to provide Afghanistan over $2 billion worth of economic aid over a ten-year span, which, if carried through, would have made Iran Kabul's biggest donor, even bigger than the Soviet Union.[19] In April 1978, Daoud also made trips to several Arab countries (Saudi Arabia, Kuwait, and Egypt), arranged for a visit by the Shah to take place in June, and announced his intention to travel to Washington to meet with President Carter. In March 1978, Afghanistan signed an economic protocol with the People's Republic of China.[20] Although the Soviets were still clearly the dominant outside power in Afghanistan, and were acknowledged as such by the United States, these attempts by Daoud to assert a more independent Afghani foreign policy certainly did not sit well with the Kremlin leadership.

The Soviets were not the only ones becoming disenchanted with Daoud. There were many groups within Afghanistan who opposed his regime. Aside from the opposition of Parcham and Khalq, there were other sectors of the population from across the political spectrum who rejected the Daoud regime's corrupt and repressive policies amid economic discontent. He tried to centralize power in a country that was practically immune to centralization. Thus, the bloody coup that overthrew Daoud in April 1978, ending the Durrani dynasty that had ruled over Afghanistan since 1747, did not come as a major shock. And one could probably have predicted Soviet involvement stemming from Moscow's increasingly negative attitude toward Daoud. Indeed, the Soviets most likely imposed a reconciliation in 1977 on the two factions of the PDPA, Khalq and Parcham.[21] Whether the Soviets actively arranged for and participated in the coup or simply gave the green light to their PDPA comrades to move when the opportunity presented itself is unclear. What is clear is that the Kremlin was definitely pleased to see Daoud go.

On April 30, 1978, a revolutionary council was decreed, with Nur Muhammad Taraki as president and prime minister. Hafizullah Amin was named foreign minister and deputy prime minister, essentially the number two position in the new regime (Amin would add the post of prime minister by March 1979, while Taraki remained president). Babrak Karmal was appointed vice president of the Revolutionary Council and also deputy prime minister, although he would be forced out of power before too long. The PDPA was basically reconstituted in the form of the new Afghani ruling regime, replete with its communist ideology and close relationship with the Soviet Union—and also the antagonisms between the three dominant personages in the leadership that had plagued the PDPA ever since its formation.

Although the new government went to some lengths to show that in fact this regime was not a puppet of the Soviet Union, many of the actions and pronouncements belied their erstwhile claims. For instance: Moscow was first to recognize the new regime; trips were made to Moscow by Afghani leaders soon after the coup amid public expressions of warmth and solidarity; in December 1978, the U.S.S.R. and Afghanistan signed a treaty of friendship and cooperation, a major sign of a tightening relationship between the Soviet Union and a client-state; the formal name of the country was changed to the Democratic Republic of Afghanistan, a traditional signal among pro-Soviet states of at least the outward veneer of a communist state; and a new red flag—in place of the partially green Islamic one—that was similar to the Soviet flag was adopted.

All the Carter administration could do to react to the April coup was express some consternation. There was little more the United States could have done considering the overwhelmingly dominant position of the Soviet Union in Afghanistan. However, the critics believe that Carter's failure to respond more forcefully to the coup led the Kremlin to conclude that Washington cared little about the course of events in Afghanistan and, in combination with subsequent instances of relative passivity, that the United States would probably not react very strongly to an actual military invasion.

The reconciliation between the Khalqis and the Parchamis, which had probably been orchestrated by Moscow prior to the coup, was short-lived. It was not long before Taraki and Amin started to replace the Parchamis within the government, including Babrak Karmal (who apparently was put in safekeeping by the Soviets until they could trot him out as the new Afghani leader following the invasion), as well as others who were suspected anticommunists. Solidarity within the ruling clique had been achieved for the time being, but at the expense of national solidarity and a number of skilled bureaucratic personnel of which the government was in short supply.

With its place secure, the regime then attempted to implement a communist-inspired political, social, economic, and even cultural, reform program that would have made Lenin proud. But it was making the Kremlin of Leonid Brezhnev extremely uneasy; in a deeply traditional, Sunni Muslim, and tribally based society, it was like trying to fit a square peg into a round hole. As Thomas Hammond states:

> There seems to be no reason to doubt that the Khalq leaders sincerely wished to institute a number of desirable and long-overdue reforms—to improve the lot of the peasants, elevate the status of women, eliminate racial discrimination, wipe out backwardness, and make Afghanistan a modern, prosperous state. But good intentions are not enough. As happened in other communist countries, the attempt to impose rapid and arbitrary change by brute force, against the wishes of the people, produced not progress but chaos, bloodshed, and civil war.[22]

Such measures as land reform, which was based on Marxist class relations that undermined the authority and economic position of local village and tribal leaders, the prohibition of certain traditional marriage arrangements, and the adoption of atheistic communist discourse and symbols in place of Islamic references fueled the opposition to the new leadership. Whatever the nature of the policies, just the attempt to centralize power and authority in Kabul engendered opposition throughout much of Afghanistan, especially outside of the major cities, areas that had become accustomed to a significant amount of autonomy from the central government over the years. As Olivier Roy stated:

> The spontaneous uprisings against the communist regime which broke out in 1978 and 1979 were directed as much against the state itself as against the Marxist government. The imposition of communism on the country may be seen as a new and even more radical phase of the penetration of the countryside by the state bureaucracy. These two dimensions, opposition to the state and the rejection of Marxism, are closely interlinked.[23]

The opposition to the government was far greater under Taraki and Amin than it had been under Daoud. The Kremlin probably did not counsel the new regime to implement these far-reaching reforms in such a force-fed manner; in the past Moscow had maintained its distance in terms of its influence upon Afghani domestic policy as long as the country was firmly within its grip. If anything, the new regime's leap toward communism displayed an independent bent on the part of Kabul that made Soviet leaders wary of what it would do next.[24]

The opposition to the Kabul regime manifested itself primarily in traditional Islam, by those who happened to also be the most disrupted by the reform policies. Uprisings in the form of a *jihad* or holy war became commonplace by the summer of 1978, and by the fall of that year, a full-scale rebellion had been ignited.[25] One of the turning points in the burgeoning civil war came in March 1979 when Afghan soldiers in Herat, Afghanistan's second largest city, joined with the rebels (*mujahideen* or holy warriors) on a rampage through the city that left hundreds of loyalist Afghan soldiers and government officials dead. In addition, a number of Soviet advisors and their families were brutally killed, dismembered, and their body parts put on display. The cathartic nature of the violence perpetrated against the Soviets clearly revealed the vehemence with which most Afghanis opposed the Soviet presence and those Afghanis who, in their view, did Moscow's bidding. The temporary loss of Herat could not but make the Kremlin nervous about the current regime's ability to quell the rebellion and restore some semblance of order.

As the rebellion grew, so did the ruthlessness with which the Afghan armed forces tried to suppress it, which, in turn, only emboldened the *mujahideen* and added to their ranks. Soon after the debacle in Herat, Amin assumed the title of prime minister from Taraki, while the latter retained his position as president and defense minister.[26] This was apparently a sign of Amin's growing strength within the Afghani hierarchy and a more assertive repression of the rebellion. However, the regime still failed to achieve its objectives. The increasing inability of the Afghani military to deal with the insurrection compelled Moscow to send more and more military advisors and military aid to Afghanistan.[27] The Kremlin's incremental military involvement

in a Third World country to prop up an unpopular, corrupt, and ineffi-
cient client-state regime was not unlike what the United States experienced in the early 1960s in South Vietnam; however, in the Afghani
case, this incremental buildup occurred over months rather than
years.

Events in Afghanistan began to unravel soon after Taraki returned
from a trip to Moscow to consult with Kremlin leaders in September
1979. The U.S. State Department had gathered information in August
which indicated that the Soviets were trying to get rid of Amin, whom
the Kremlin saw as the heart of the problem. There is some disagreement about exactly what happened on September 14 and 15, but
according to most accounts, Taraki, apparently at the behest of the
Soviet Union (and possibly the Soviet ambassador to Afghanistan,
Alexander Puzanov), arranged a meeting in order to ambush Amin. In
a "shoot-out" at the People's Palace in Kabul, Amin emerged
unscathed, but he immediately turned his sights on Taraki, stripping
him of authority and assuming his offices on September 16. Taraki was
never heard from again; according to some reports he was executed in
early October, although the official explanation was that he died of a
long-standing serious illness.

Relations between the Soviet Union and Amin clearly deteriorated
after this episode, as the Afghani leader concluded that the Soviets
were definitely out to eliminate him. Knowing this, the Soviets
became even more concerned that Amin would make entreaties to the
United States for protection and possibly some leverage with Moscow.
Some diplomatic approaches were initiated by U.S. officials toward
Amin, but nothing really came of them, and despite claims by the
Soviets that Amin was a CIA agent, Washington was unable and/or
unwilling to insert itself into the chaotic Afghani political landscape.[28]
Arnold sums up the deteriorating environment as follows:

> His position was not an enviable one. Only about half of his army's nor-
> mal officer corps strength of eight thousand remained; the rest had been
> killed or had gone over to the rebels. Mutinies in his forces had become
> commonplace. The PDPA, splintered by the ex-communication of the
> Parchamis in 1978, was now splitting again as Amin's supporters ranged
> against those of Taraki. Insurgency was everywhere; the government

could control individual cities by dispatching its dwindling military forces to the most critical danger points, but not even Kabul was safe from insurgent attacks and military rebellions. Afghanistan's economy was in a shambles. And looming over other considerations was the all-too-evident military solution that the USSR might seek to impose if the Afghans failed to set their own house in order.[29]

Making Soviet military intervention all too evident was the foreboding presence in Afghanistan from August through October 1979 of General Alexander Pavlovskii, the commander in chief of Soviet ground forces and deputy minister of defense. He was experienced in this type of situation, for he had been the head of Soviet ground troops that invaded Czechoslovakia in 1968.

The presence of General Pavlovskii suggests that by late summer, the Kremlin was seriously considering an invasion of Afghanistan and planning accordingly. Perhaps what Moscow wanted most from Amin was an official invitation for Soviet military intervention to restore order. This would lessen any international outcry, at least from the Soviet perspective, against the military action, and it would be in official accordance with Afghan-Soviet agreements, primarily the 1978 Treaty of Friendship and Cooperation. But Amin would not issue the invitation, probably because he knew he would be removed once the Soviets entered Afghanistan, a suspicion that would prove correct when the actual invasion occurred. To the Soviets, this was perhaps the last straw, and it may have convinced any doubters in the Kremlin that Amin was not sufficiently subservient and had to go.

An official request for Soviet intervention was eventually made by the Afghani government on December 27, but it was several days *after* Soviet military forces had already entered Afghani territory en masse—and it was not made by Amin, but by his replacement, Babrak Karmal, who had been kept in cold storage by the Kremlin for just this occasion. Amin and several members of his family were killed by Soviet special forces on the night of December 27, and then Karmal made the "request."[30] The massive nature of the invasion (more than 80,000 troops with equally impressive supporting materiel) not only indicated the urgency felt by the Kremlin but also was calculated to ensure victory over the rebels and any Afghani elements of the armed forces. It was also most likely intended to advertise the power of the Soviet Union to any other client states that might have similar rebellious tendencies and to deter any outside parties from even entertaining the idea of direct military intervention to counter the Soviet blitzkrieg.

It is clear from these events that Afghanistan was very important to the Soviet Union. The rationale for the invasion usually combines a panoply of offensive and defensive reasons. Among them, the most frequently stated explanations are the following.

1. Since the Soviet Union has been invaded on numerous occasions in modern history, most destructively in World War II, it has had a natural defensive paranoia that produced in the postwar period the need for friendly states along its borders to act as a kind of buffer between itself and its real and perceived enemies. This buffer manifested itself initially in Eastern Europe with the Warsaw Pact countries, since the primary threat was seen to be the United States and Western Europe as embodied in NATO. However, with the emergence of China as a threat to the south of the Soviet Union and with increasing Western interests in the oil-rich Persian Gulf, this buffer zone was extended to include Afghanistan; it had to remain within the Soviet orbit and be obedient to Kremlin designs. The Carter administration's rapprochement with China, highlighted by the establishment of diplomatic relations in January 1979, only exacerbated the Soviet fear of being boxed in by the enemy.

2. The Kremlin feared that the unrest in Afghanistan could spread to the Muslim-populated Soviet republics of south-central Asia, such as Uzbekistan, Turkmenistan, and Tajikistan, enticing like-minded Muslim groups clamoring for more autonomy or outright independence from Soviet rule. The invasion would supposedly head this off before it had a chance to cross borders and at the same time send a strong message in order to deter any such outbreaks in other parts of the Soviet empire. In actuality, the Soviet invasion only increased the sympathies of Muslims in Soviet republics toward their Afghani coreligionists and enhanced the likelihood of unrest spreading across the border.

3. There was serious concern in the Kremlin that if the U.S.S.R. did not act soon, or if it decided to let the civil war play itself out, Amin

would fall from power and be replaced by an anti-Soviet Islamic fundamentalist regime that would establish close relations with countries such as Iran, Pakistan, and possibly even the United States.[31] With so much of the Soviet military committed to the long border with China, the Kremlin felt it could ill afford to have another hostile country along its borders requiring an expanded military defense presence and possibly acting as a bridgehead to foment unrest in the Muslim areas of the Soviet Union.

4. The Soviet Union believed it had the right to intervene in order to preserve the sanctity of the communist bloc, as it did in Czechoslovakia in 1968. The so-called Brezhnev Doctrine held that once a state became communist, it would always remain communist, lest any precedent be set for reversing the Marxist-Leninist process.[32]

5. Traditional Czarist and Soviet expansionism has also been put forward as a more offensive-minded rationale for the invasion. According to this view, the invasion of 1979 was simply the latest in a series of Soviet invasions of Afghanistan in the twentieth century, and the question that should be asked is not why the U.S.S.R. invaded in 1979 but why it had not done so earlier. With its position in Afghanistan secure, the Soviets could then, at the very least, foment instability for U.S.-supported regimes in south Asia and in the Persian Gulf region (similar to what Czarist Russia did to the British in India in the nineteenth century). At most, the Soviets could extend their influence through military intimidation, if not direct military action, toward the Persian Gulf, where approximately two-thirds of the world's known oil reserves are located. It was this possibility that elicited the Carter Doctrine in January 1980, which anointed the Persian Gulf as a vital interest of the United States that would be defended by any means necessary.

6. The weakness of the U.S. response at a number of different levels may have contributed significantly to the Kremlin belief that it could get away with the invasion without too much damage to its international stature and to its relationship with the United States. Contributing to this belief was the perceived failure of Washington to stand by and support its ally, the Shah of Iran, when he was confronted by the Khomeini-led opposition. On top of this, the relative weakness of the U.S. response to the taking of the fifty-two American

embassy personnel as hostages by Iranian revolutionaries in early November 1979 may have reinforced the view that Carter would not respond forcefully to a Soviet invasion of Afghanistan. In addition, there were clear signals that the Soviets were preparing for a possible invasion of Afghanistan by the fall of 1979, and yet the Carter administration did virtually nothing to attach any seriousness to the situation or convey what the consequences might be if the Soviets did invade. No clear public warnings were delivered (until it was much too late) that might have at least made the Kremlin think twice about invading its southern neighbor. To the Soviet leadership in Moscow, it seemed that the United States was still hamstrung by the Vietnam syndrome and did not have any appetite for military confrontation in far-flung places.[33] The fact that the Shah was gone and that, after the hostage crisis, U.S.-Iranian relations were totally severed must have added to the confidence of the Kremlin leadership that the United States not only would not but now, without assets in Iran, could not do anything to impede the invasion.

Nevertheless, the invasion, contrary to what the Soviets had probably thought, did produce a swift and serious response from the United States. More importantly, however, the Soviets would indeed become enmeshed in their own Vietnam quagmire, with significant repercussions regionally and immense consequences globally.

3

Future Past

Perhaps not enough time has passed to soberly examine the effects of the year 1979. It seems, however, that not a day goes by when there is not something in the news on at least one of the following topics: the Middle East peace process, Russian activities in the south-central portions of their country, Islamic "extremist" groups, Saddam Hussein's tug-of-war over sanctions with the United Nations, political change in or perceived threats from Iran, and heightened tensions between Pakistan and India. Every one of these news stories can be traced to events that transpired in 1979. Some might postpone an examination of these events until more weight is added to the history that would determine their significance. It is my contention, however, that we need not wait. Enough history, enough primary effects have occurred since 1979 to allow a subjective annualization.

Although such events seem very distinct now, in five hundred years, if not sooner, historical texts might very well refer to the 1979 Egyptian-Israeli peace treaty, the 1993 Israeli-PLO accords, and the 1994 Israeli-Jordanian treaty (and whatever Arab-Israeli treaties lie ahead) in the same sentence. Similarly, the Iranian revolution, the Iran-Iraq war, and the Persian Gulf crisis and war will most likely be mentioned in the same breath. This all may be a historian's folly—typically esoteric historical legerdemain. But it is also historical curiosity.[1] We have a natural inclination to want to know when things began or what caused what to happen—the turning points in history. If possible, we like things neatly categorized. The fact that we are able to at least surmise the importance of a particular year so soon after it happened, in relative historical terms, may just reinforce the argument for its significance. The repercussions of the events that occurred in the Middle East in 1979 have been felt in such a widespread and influential manner and in such a short period of time that, in my opinion, there already exist copious amounts of history. The historical interconnections will become apparent, both in a horizontal and a vertical sense. The links in the chain from important events and situations today can be clearly traced backward in time to their points of origin in the events of 1979—the past as future for the year 1979.

The Iranian Revolution

As stated in Chapter 2, the culmination of the Iranian revolution occurred in February 1979, when the Ayatollah Khomeini arrived in Teheran after fifteen years of exile and proclaimed the Islamic Republic of Iran, replacing the U.S.-supported monarchy of the Shah of Iran, Muhammad Reza Pahlavi. As events would show, this change severely disrupted the balance of power in and stability of the Persian Gulf region, an area that contains approximately two-thirds of the world's known oil reserves. This fact alone preordained that an event of this magnitude would draw the attention of the international community.

Even though the Iranian revolution was a Shiite Muslim revolution, Muslims across the Middle East, both Sunni and Shiite, who had become disaffected with secular pan-Arab nationalism and state-building since the effectual death of Nasserist pan-Arabism in the 1967 Arab-Israeli war, hailed the event as a true harbinger of things to come. No longer would the Islamic world have to kowtow to the West and accept the inevitability of Israel. Islam's cultural identity and heritage need not be replaced by Western cultural and economic imperialism. The Islamists who survived the secular Arab nationalist era of the 1950s, 1960s, and 1970s could now point with pride to a successful example of religious revolution and Islamic rule in the modern era to combat the internal and external threats to society. If the defeat of Nasserism and secular Arab nationalism in the 1967 Arab-Israeli war created the opening for a resuscitation of Islamism, the Iranian revolution provided the direction and momentum for Islamist groups. Pan-

Islamism would replace pan-Arabism, and if successful, a *Pax Islamica* would reign over the region, with Iran showing the way.

Would Islamic extremism have continued to grow and expand if the Iranian revolution had not occurred? With the continuing exhaustion of the state in the Arab world in political and economic terms, the answer is most certainly yes. Would the Islamic alternative and the adoption of dramatic methodologies to implement this alternative have become as popular or threatening if the revolution had not occurred? The answer to this is most certainly no. This would have been the case even if the new Islamic Republic in Iran had simply served as an example and turned inward and concentrated on domestic development and internal purification. But with a charismatic and firebrand demagogue such as Khomeini calling on the export of the Islamic revolution, the liberation of Jerusalem, and a confrontation against the Great Satan, the United States, the Middle East would never be the same. In an attempt to portray the revolution as an Islamic rather than simply an Iranian one, the Khomeini regime immediately engaged itself in a variety of issues close to the heart of all Arabs, namely, the Palestinian problem. Symbolically driving this point home was the fact that within about a week after the success of the revolution in February, the Khomeini regime closed down the Israeli embassy in Teheran and gave it to the PLO and Yasir Arafat, who was visiting Iran at the time.[2]

The impact of the revolution was immediately felt in the region. Regimes in the Persian Gulf squirmed nervously over the potential domestic repercussions. In Iraq, the secular, Sunni, Ba'thist ruling party of Saddam Hussein saw the revolution as both a threat and an opportunity. The revolution created a threat in that the majority of the population in Iraq was Shiite and, therefore, possibly susceptible to Iranian démarches to overthrow a regime that was neither appropriately religious nor adequately representative. It was an opportunity in that Iran was seen as vulnerable due to the domestic turmoil in the aftermath of the revolution as the parties that formed the coalition opposed to the Shah jockeyed for position within the new government. In addition, Saddam was cognizant of the fact that the Iranian armed forces had been depleted as a result of the change of power and were in substantial disarray (and soon to be clearly bereft of American military support). The situation might just be the conduit for Saddam to achieve his regional hegemonic ambitions.

The rest of the Gulf Arab states—Saudi Arabia, Kuwait, United Arab Emirates, Qatar, Bahrain, and Oman—were equally concerned about this new threat emanating from the east. This was particularly true of states that had substantial Shiite minority populations (Saudi Arabia and Kuwait) and Bahrain, a country that, not unlike Iraq, was (and still is) a majority Shiite state ruled by a Sunni minority regime. It did not take long for this threat to manifest itself in the region. On November 20, 1979, 225 well-armed Islamic militants took control of the Grand Mosque in Mecca, Saudi Arabia, the holiest site in all of Islam. Even though the militants were, by and large, Sunnis, the Iranian revolution had galvanized Islamists throughout the Middle East to take the next step toward action against what they perceived as their combined enemies: the West, Israel, and co-opted and sycophantic Muslims.[3]

This was a very embarrassing episode for the Saudi monarchy, since the Al Saud are officially the Guardians of the Two Holy Places (Mecca and Medina), and a significant part of their legitimacy stems from the family's control and upkeep of the shrines as well as the annual pilgrimage or *hajj*. The militants were led by a Saudi man by the name of Juhayman bin Muhammad bin Sayf al-Utaiba, who had been openly agitating against the Saudi regime for several years, demanding a more pure application of Saudi Arabia's Wahhabi strain of Sunni Islam. In fact, the preoccupation of the Saudi regime with the perceived rising threat of Khomeinism might have resulted in the Saudi security services paying relatively little attention to homegrown opposition movements.[4] The apparent inability of the Saudi monarchy to protect the Grand Mosque in the face of continuing accusations of corruption and subservience to the United States amounted to a very serious moment of vulnerability for the Saudi ruling regime. Only after an official religious ruling *(fatwa)* from the Grand Mufti in Riyadh did the regime attempt to retake the shrine through cautious force so as not to damage the structure itself, which only made it that much more difficult to overrun the militants. The resulting blood spilt in Islam's holiest site almost shook the monarchy to the ground.[5] However, it was only a foreshadowing of the constant problems Saudi Arabia would have with pilgrims (especially from Iran) during the course of the

1980s, as Mecca became the target for political ire over Saudi Arabia's overt backing of Baghdad in the Iran-Iraq war.

Only a month later, another disturbance occurred that shook the Saudi regime and indicated to all interested observers that the reverberations from the Iranian revolution would be more than just fitful. The Shiite minority in Saudi Arabia lives, for the most part, in the northeast portion of the country in the al-Hasa region, where most of the active oil reserves in the country are located. The relationship is not coincidental; the Shiite population constitutes the lion's share of oil field laborers. Overworked, underpaid, and underprivileged, the Shiites needed only a spark to cathartically unleash their frustration against the regime. That spark was the annual *ashura* celebration during the Islamic month of Muharram, which happened to fall in December that year. This event, or passion play, to be more precise, commemorates the martyrdom of the Imam Hussein, the grandson of the prophet Muhammad and one of the central figures in Shiite Islam, in 680 C.E. on the plains outside of Karbala in present-day Iraq (it occurred, according to Shiite theology, on the tenth day of Muharram—ten in Arabic is *ashura*). It is a highly emotional affair, as many Shiite youths flagellate and bloody themselves in order to emulate and empathize with the Imam Hussein at Karbala 1300 years earlier. With the Iranian revolution still burning in the hearts of many Shiites and with the Grand Mosque episode still fresh in their minds, the emotional atmosphere produced by the *ashura* celebration naturally led to riots amid loud support for the Ayatollah Khomeini. Again, the Saudi regime had to use force to put down the disturbances—and Saddam Hussein looked on with increasing consternation.[6]

The Iranian revolution also presented to Saddam Hussein an opportunity. Already claiming a leadership position in the Arab world in the wake of Egypt's peace treaty with Israel (evidenced by the fact that the two emergency Arab League summit meetings to condemn Egypt and assess the new circumstances—one held after Camp David and the other following the signing of the treaty in March 1979—were held in Baghdad), Saddam leveraged this newfound influence into the position of protector of the Arab world against Persian and radical (Shiite) Islamic extremism and expansionism. In one fell swoop, Iraq could fill two vacuums of power in the Middle East—one in the Arab world, and implicitly in the Arab-Israeli arena, created by Egypt's departure and the other in the Persian Gulf arena brought about by the fall of the Shah. As a sign of Saddam's heightened ambitions, he nudged aside President Hasan al-Bakr (resigning officially due to "ill health") and assumed the position of president himself on July 16, 1979. Although he had been the strongman behind Hasan for years, Saddam was clearly now coming out of the shadows. Almost immediately Saddam showed his stripes, as prominent members of the Revolutionary Command Council (RCC) were arrested and later executed on August 8. Many other officials in the government and in the military were also executed or imprisoned on charges of "conspiracy against the party and revolution."[7] He was now in position to implement his agenda.

Iran was, to most observers, vulnerable. Ayatollah Khomeini had not yet solidified his position as supreme ruler, and it was still unclear how Islamic this new republic was going to be. Violence in Iran had become so commonplace that "Tonight Show" host Johnny Carson seemed to always have some sort of a joke in his opening monologue referring to the bombs frequently going off in Teheran, reflecting the political infighting among the coalition partners that had overthrown the Shah. With all the disarray within the regime and at least as much disruption within the Iranian military following the exiles, purges, defections, and executions that came in the wake of the revolution, it seemed that with only a slight push Iran would topple altogether. Paramount in Saddam's calculations on taking advantage of this situation was making sure the United States would not come to Iran's aid.[8]

U.S. isolation from Iran became assured on November 4, 1979, when Revolutionary Guards, the shock troops of Khomeini's revolution, stormed the American embassy in Teheran and took ninety persons, including sixty-three Americans, hostage (fifty-two Americans would be held for 444 days). Washington, inter alia, broke off relations with Iran, froze Iranian assets in the United States, and worked to isolate Iran within the international community, thus inaugurating a period of extreme hostility between the two countries.[9] More importantly, from Saddam Hussein's perspective, this meant that the mostly American-supplied Iranian military would not be able to easily obtain spare parts, ammunition, or other complementary equipment from

American sources. Bereft of these materials and many of the military personnel trained to use the equipment, the multibillion-dollar U.S.-supplied military arsenal the Shah had amassed would be more vestigial than daunting.

All of these new circumstances indicated to Saddam Hussein a unique opportunity with a possible fabulous payoff: the elimination of the threat from Iran and the attainment of personal and national ambitions of leadership in the Middle East. With this in mind, Iraq attacked southwestern Iran in September 1980, and the eight-year Iran-Iraq war was on.

So momentous was the Iranian revolution that even some of its direct repercussions became significant independent variables in and of themselves. The Iranian hostage crisis is a case in point. The United States had been relatively unscathed by international terrorism. Very few Americans had been directly or indirectly affected by terrorist actions. The term "hostage" was more known in reference to being held by "fortune" rather than by international terrorists or politically driven groups. Yet the Iranian revolution introduced the United States to a new era and a heightened level of anti-Americanism and political extremism. The psychological barriers and the taboo of striking directly at America seemed to have been lifted, inaugurating a period of Middle East terrorist activity that became inexorably linked with Middle East politics and conflicts from Beirut and Cairo to the Persian Gulf and South Asia. And the more the United States became involved in the region diplomatically and/or militarily, the more it became a target. Although the storming of the American embassy and the taking of hostages was as much a function of internal power-play politics within the faction-ridden Teheran regime as a pure act of anti-Americanism, its repercussions would have at least as much impact on domestic politics in the United States as they did in Iran.

As has often been stated, the Carter administration became hostage to the hostage situation. The inability of the Carter administration to either obtain the release of the hostages or rescue them enhanced the appearance of American weakness, a national complex that the country was still trying to shed in the aftermath of Vietnam. And world events, such as the burning of the American embassy in Islamabad shortly after the Mecca incident, the assassination of the U.S. ambassador in Afghanistan earlier in the year, and most importantly, the Soviet invasion of Afghanistan in December 1979 made the United States seem impotent in the face of renewed Soviet aggression and global hostility toward Washington.

The Carter administration had seriously contemplated military action to either directly free the hostages or pressure the Iranian government to force their release soon after the actual hostage-taking in November. However, the Soviet invasion of Afghanistan the following month changed the calculations dramatically. Washington did not want to add to the instability in the Persian Gulf region caused by the Soviet incursion by forcing a military showdown with Iran (a decision with which Washington's Arab allies in the Gulf concurred). In addition, the Soviet invasion had perforce placed the United States and Iran on the same side with remarkably similar objectives with regard to the situation in Afghanistan. It was hoped that Teheran would realize the convergence of security interests that would in turn lead to a relatively precipitant diplomatic resolution to the hostage crisis.

When a diplomatic resolution did not materialize, concurrent with the languishing popularity of the administration domestically, President Carter made the fateful decision to attempt a daring rescue in April 1979, while the hostages were reportedly still kept largely together in one location. The disastrous failure of the Desert One action, however, with loss of American lives and the abandoning of several helicopters in the Iranian desert, only added to the appearance of American impotence and to the ineptitude of the administration itself, and perhaps most important, made it that much more difficult to negotiate the hostages' release in coming months (or plan another rescue attempt since the hostages were subsequently dispersed).[10]

To say that the hostage crisis significantly hurt Carter's chances for reelection is quite the understatement. With the cold war against the Soviets seemingly starting anew, the last thing Americans wanted was a weakened president who (along with his secretary of state, Cyrus Vance) had consistently emphasized human rights and negotiations over strategic calculations and military force. The hostage crisis had significantly helped mold the national psyche into yearning for a strong-willed American patriot who would repair America's image abroad and rebuild the military into a positive instrument of foreign policy. Arch-conservative Ronald Reagan's landslide victory in the 1980 presidential election was the natural response. The crowning blow to Carter delivered by Teheran was the fact that the hostages were released just minutes after Reagan was inaugurated president on January 20, 1981, 444 days after they had been taken.

In Iran, the hostage ordeal helped solidify the power of Ayatollah Khomeini and his radical Islamist faction. His influence over the hostage-taking youths and his manipulation of the diplomatic process clearly popularized his position during this volcanic period of the revolution, whereas the more moderate officials in the regime, such as the "lay" Islamic leaders Abolhasan Bani-Sadr, the first president of the new Islamic Republic, Sadeq Ghotbzadeh, and Ibrahim Yazdi, were seen to be relatively powerless. Eventually they would be cast aside, cementing the Islamist theocratic nature of the regime *(hukumat islami)* and the position of Khomeini as the Supreme Guide.[11]

The success of the Iranian revolution galvanized Islamists the world over. The rise of Khomeini obviously had a direct effect, as noted previously, on the takeover of the Grand Mosque in Mecca, the riots by Shiites in the eastern oil fields in Saudi Arabia, and, of course, the hostage crisis. Iran also became the direct sponsor of Hizbullah (the Party of God), a Shiite Muslim group that arose in South Lebanon as a result of the Israeli invasion of Lebanon in 1982 (particularly Israel's decision to stay on and establish a security zone in South Lebanon).[12] The Israeli invasion of Lebanon was a direct result of the Egyptian-Israeli peace treaty of 1979, as will be shown later in this chapter.[13] Hizbullah played a prominent role in the hostage-taking and assassinations of Westerners and hijackings in and around Beirut throughout much of the 1980s. The Iranian connection with Hizbullah also led directly to the infamous Iran-Contra affair exposed in late 1986 by a Lebanese newspaper. Hizbullah was, and still is, also supported by Syria, a relationship that, in the beginning, increased Syria's ability to disrupt Israeli and American attempts to exclude Damascus from its power position in Lebanon following the Israeli invasion. And in recent years, Syria's support of the Shiite group has enhanced its leverage with regard to negotiations dealing with a hoped-for Israeli withdrawal from the Golan Heights.

As is well known, the Iran-Contra affair was the Reagan administration's attempt to sell arms to the Khomeini regime in Iran (which
was obviously desperate for American weaponry and ammunition by
that point in its war with Iraq) in return for utilizing its influence with
Hizbullah in Lebanon, pressuring it to free American hostages. This
was in contravention of Washington's own Operation Staunch, which
was (an attempt at) a worldwide arms embargo of Iran. The money
paid by the regime in Teheran for the arms was then funneled illegally to the U.S.-supported Contras in Nicaragua to support their
attempts to overthrow the Marxist Sandinista regime in Managua.
This was in direct violation of legislation passed by Congress that cut
off covert assistance to the Contras.[14]

The irony in this whole episode is rampant. First of all, the Reagan
administration came to office committed to a policy of not dealing
with terrorists and not letting any hostage situation captivate the
White House—in direct reaction to the failure of the Carter administration's foibles in Iran. Second, the idea of dealing with so-called moderate elements in Teheran in an arms-for-hostages deal originated with
the Israelis. Despite the animosity emanating from Teheran toward
the Jewish state (refrained with the cry of "liberating Jerusalem"),
Israel had established a secret channel with Teheran, which, as stated
earlier, was desperate to receive arms from anyone, particularly a military whose weaponry was somewhat compatible with American
weaponry. From Israel's perspective, the traditional Arab proverb
"the enemy of my enemy is my friend" held true in this instance, as the
common foes of Iraq made for strange bedfellows. Yet, it was the Israeli
invasion in 1982 that created the environment for the birth of
Hizbullah (as well as other anti-American and anti-Israeli groups in
Lebanon) and the series of kidnappings and killings. The scandal
rocked the Reagan administration and launched a series of investiga-
tions and hearings. With the subsequent 1983 bombing of the marine
barracks in Beirut, which resulted in 241 deaths and the eventual U.S.
withdrawal from the Lebanese quagmire by early 1984, the Reagan
administration, for most of the remainder of its term, essentially withdrew from an active role in the Arab-Israeli arena.

The administration did pursue diplomatic initiatives toward the end
of its tenure in office, but this was primarily in reaction to PLO

Chairman Yasir Arafat's decision in late 1988 to finally recognize Israel, accept UN Security Council Resolution 242, and renounce terrorism. This shift allowed the Reagan administration to begin a dialogue with PLO officials, which, in the end, did not progress substantially before the presidential administration of George Bush took office in January 1989 and events were overtaken by the Gulf crisis and war of 1990–1991. Again, the combination of Egypt's absence in the inter-Arab arena as a result of the peace treaty with Israel, the Israeli invasion of Lebanon, and the Iran-Iraq war, all of which indelibly split the Arab world into a number of competing camps, created an environment that led to a somewhat disinterested Reagan administration by the end of 1986. The lack of movement on the Palestinian issue (reinforced by the Arab League summit meeting held in Amman, Jordan, in November 1987, which for the first time relegated the Palestinian issue to a secondary status on the agenda in light of the Iran-Iraq war) increased the frustration of the Palestinians living in the West Bank and Gaza Strip, leading directly to the *intifada* or uprising that began in December 1987. This, in turn, compelled Arafat to moderate the PLO's position before the irrelevance portended by its expulsion from Lebanon in 1982 and essential exile in Tunisia became cemented by the Palestinians in the occupied territories taking matters into their own hands.

The Iran-Contra affair, however, had the opposite effect in the Persian Gulf arena. The Arab allies of the United States in the Persian Gulf, who had been overtly supporting Iraq to varying degrees in its war with Iran, were obviously shocked and dismayed by the revelations of the arms-for-hostages deal. The United States seemed to be playing both sides of the fence. The Reagan administration's need to regain credibility in the eyes of its Arab friends significantly influenced its decision to begin reflagging Kuwaiti oil tankers under U.S. flags in June 1987, following the initiation of the so-called tanker war by Iraq and the subsequent response by Iran against those tankers, particularly Kuwaiti registered ones that were carrying Iraqi oil. The United States thus established a direct military presence in the Persian Gulf, which overtly placed Washington on Iraq's side in the Iran-Iraq war, leading to a number of military confrontations with Iranian forces in Gulf waters and solidifying a (hoped-for) strategic partnership with

Saddam Hussein. Washington was blinded into thinking Iraq could assume Iran's position under the Shah as America's gendarme of the Gulf. As Gary Sick states, the reflagging operation

> was a fundamental turning point. For the first time since World War II, the United States assumed an operational role in the defense of the Persian Gulf. . . . President Reagan's military intervention thus confirmed President Carter's assertion that the Gulf was of vital interest to the United States and that the United States was prepared to use military force in pursuit of that interest. Although the Carter Doctrine [announced in January 1980] addressed the prospective threat from the Soviet Union [in reaction to the Soviet invasion of Afghanistan in December 1979], its first major implementation involved a regional state, anticipating the massive international coalition that repelled Iraq's occupation of Kuwait.[15]

All of this stemmed directly from the Iranian revolution. The Islamist drive fueled by Khomeini that led to Hizbullah and ultimately to Iran-Contra and subsequent events also was felt elsewhere in the Middle East. The success of the revolution and the antipathy toward Israel overtly on display in Teheran galvanized growing Islamist opposition in Egypt toward Anwar Sadat's regime, which was seen by Egyptian Islamists as having betrayed Islam by signing a peace treaty with Israel and for embracing the West politically, militarily, economically, and culturally. It is doubtful that the assassination of Sadat by the Islamic Jihad organization on October 6, 1981, the anniversary of the initiation of the 1973 Arab-Israeli war, would have occurred when it did if not for the inspiration from Teheran. Indeed, there were groups in Egypt that needed no reinforcement from Iran to hate the peace treaty, Sadat, and all he stood for—and attempt to kill him—but the revolution tended to "mainstream" Islamist dissent, popularizing it and generating the buildup of willing recruits, if not martyrs, for the cause in both Sunni and Shiite circles.[16]

In combination with a host of other factors, especially socioeconomic discontent, perceived cultural imperialism, and globalization, significant, serious, and militant Islamist movements sprang up across the region, threatening regime survival and eliciting government responses that ranged from the militarily extreme (the deaths of 20,000–40,000 in Hama in Syria in 1982) to the prudently political (in Jordan and Kuwait, for example, where Islamist opposition parties were legalized and allowed to enter parliament, thus, in the end, moderating the position of many from clamoring to overthrow the government to wanting to bring about peaceful change from within) to the ill-advised (for instance, the decision by the Algerian military to cancel the January 1992 parliamentary elections in which the Islamist party, the Islamic Salvation Front, was poised to win the largest bloc, thus initiating a bloody civil war that still rages on and has cost 75,000–100,000 lives).[17]

Although many of the Islamist groups that arose in the 1980s have splintered into unrecognizable factions or have been successfully contained by the repressive apparatuses of a number of regimes, other variants have arisen, many transnational in nature, particularly the group associated with Osama bin Laden (al-Qaida), which, ironically, is now actually opposed to the regime in Teheran. Islamist opposition has obviously taken on new characteristics, followers, and causes since 1979, affected as they have been by a host of intervening events since that time, but it is also clear that none of it could have taken noticeable shape without the Iranian revolution lifting the bar to a whole different level. Indeed, such has been the course of events within this sphere of activity that it has influenced leading scholars, such as Samuel Huntington, to (mistakenly in my opinion) conclude that there exists a "clash of civilizations" along the fault line between Christian civilization and Islamic civilization. The Iranian revolution plays an important role in the calculations of those who adhere to this point of view, which, unfortunately, if advocated by too many on either side of the so-called divide, might become a self-fulfilling prophecy.[18]

The most direct and immediately significant repercussion of the Iranian revolution was, of course, the Iran-Iraq war, which lasted from September 1980, when Iraq invaded Iran, to August 1988, when Iran reluctantly agreed to a UN-brokered cease-fire. The war was less important in and of itself, as it settled down into trench warfare within a year with scant movement on either side of the front for most of the conflict, but more because of its tangential effects.

As previously mentioned, Saddam Hussein ordered the invasion for defensive and offensive reasons. Most of all, he saw an opportunity—Iran was vulnerable and isolated, and the regional and international situation seemed to be in Iraq's favor. The war lasted as long as it did, with more than a million casualties, for a number of reasons.

1. The advantages of one country were offset by the advantages of the other. That is, Iran's population advantage (approximately 55–60 million to Iraq's 17–20 million) was offset by Iraq's technological advantage in military hardware, especially since Iran did not have access to American resupply and Iraq continued to receive materiel from the Soviet Union and France.[19]

2. The international community and even the countries in the region itself were not terribly motivated to end the war any time soon. Indeed, Washington and Moscow were primarily interested in making sure the conflict remained insulated and did not escalate into a super-power confrontation (especially with the Soviets mired in Afghanistan). Evidence often given to support this is the fact that the UN Security Council waited a whole week to discuss the Iraqi invasion. It seems that Iran's isolation, accelerated internationally by the hostage crisis, was coming home to haunt Teheran, and having the Khomeini regime cut down to size was not inconsistent with the wishes of a number of countries. Additionally, the Arab Gulf countries were not at all unhappy to see Iran and Iraq occupied with each other and weakening over the course of time. Because Iran was more of an immediate threat, the Arab Gulf states were compelled to monetarily support Iraq for most of the war. But they also were cognizant of the ambitions of Saddam Hussein and were fearful of his attempts to translate these ambitions into an attempted hegemonic position in the Gulf, especially if he emerged victorious—a fear that was confirmed when Iraq invaded Kuwait in 1990.

3. A host of miscalculations on both sides prolonged the conflict. Iraq attacked southwestern Iran not only for geographical and strategic reasons but also because that part of the country was host to the majority of Iran's Arab minority. Indeed, the Arabs living there call it Arabistan, instead of the official name of this province, Khuzistan. Saddam Hussein hoped that the Arabs in Iran would support his invasion, making his putsch that much more effective and depleting Iran's

ability to counterattack.[20] Unfortunately for Baghdad, the Arabs in Khuzistan were largely ambivalent to the outcome. Iraq's strategic limitations probably would have forced it to draw back its initial offensive anyhow, but the failure of the Arabs in Iran to come to Iraq's aid at this point made a swift knock-out punch all but impossible. Similarly, when Iran went on the offensive in 1982, it too thought that "fellow travelers" in enemy territory would support its cause, in this case, the Shiite Arab Muslim majority in Iraq, most of whom lived in the southern part of Iraq toward the Iranian border. Again, however, a combatant had badly miscalculated. Although there were certainly some groups of Shiite Arabs that in fact did support Teheran actively, the expected en masse Shiite uprising never materialized, primarily because of the effective repressive apparatus of the Baghdadi regime and the distaste many, mostly secularized, Iraqi Shiites had for Khomeini's brand of Shiism and theocratic regime.

4. The Manichean ideological opposition of the regimes (secular Arab versus Islamist Persian) and the personal animus and mutual recriminations and boasts invested in the war by the two leaders, which only grew as the war dragged on, greatly complicated attempts at diplomatic resolution throughout the conflagration. In addition, it seemed that anytime one side or the other gained a bit of an advantage in military terms, instead of utilizing that advantage to achieve immediate political results, it was seen as an opportunity to press for more in order to obtain full, rather than partial, war aims.

By 1982, Iran had beaten back Iraq's initial attack and had gone on the offensive. Teheran, trying to take advantage of its superior numbers, established multiple fronts against the Iraqis, hoping to extend Iraqi forces beyond their defensive capacity and to wear down Baghdad through attrition: in the north (with the help of anti-Saddam Iraqi Kurds), in the center toward Baghdad, and in the south toward Basra.

To the extent that Iraq had a strategy after 1982, Baghdad wanted to internationalize the conflict by bringing in the superpowers, especially the United States, so that they could exert pressure on Iran to cease and desist. Iraq would eventually accomplish this through its initiation of the tanker war in the Persian Gulf, but as stated previously, direct American involvement with the reflagging of Kuwaiti tankers was as much a political decision in response to the repercussions of the Iran-Contra affair as a strategic decision to overtly back Iraq. In addition, the Kuwaitis had deftly played the superpowers against one another, having gone to Moscow when Washington at first displayed some reluctance to the reflagging plan. After the Kremlin agreed to reflag some tankers, the United States then wholeheartedly came in with its buffeted offer to reflag Kuwaiti tankers. Other than internationalizing the conflict, Baghdad was simply hoping to hang on as long as possible until the octogenarian Khomeini died, which, unfortunately for the Iraqis, did not come soon enough (the Ayatollah passed away in 1989, almost a year after the war ended).

Indeed, it was the arms provided to Iran in the arms-for-hostages deal that significantly elevated Teheran's ability to launch a major offensive in 1986. With the reorganization of its military structure, which placed decisionmaking with the professional soldiery rather than with the militarily inexperienced revolutionary guards, the offensive was very successful. Iran took the Fao (Faw) Peninsula, thus cutting Iraq off from the Persian Gulf, and threatened to take Basra, Iraq's second largest city.

With the embarrassing revelation of the Iran-Contra affair and the existing desire not to see Iran victorious in this war, the United States was openly supporting Iraq, most ostentatiously displayed by the reflagging operation. In fact, Washington had reestablished diplomatic relations with Iraq (broken off since 1967) in late 1984, clearly betraying the pro-Iraqi disposition of the Reagan administration. There were some in policy circles who were advocating building up Saddam Hussein as the next "gendarme" of the Gulf—taking the place of the fallen Shah—and continuing the balance of power approach to the region. Furthermore, there were more than a few who suggested that Saddam Hussein could additionally take the place of Anwar Sadat and finish what the Egyptian president was unable to accomplish, that is, lead a moderate Arab consensus into a comprehensive peace with Israel. It seems preposterous now, considering the extremely antagonistic relationship between Iraq and the United States since the Gulf war, but at the time, Khomeinism was the point of focus, and Iran was at least as ostracized and held in as much contempt by Washington as Iraq has been in recent years. The common threat emanating from Iran after 1979 brought Baghdad and Washington closer together, establishing the foundation of the strategic relationship toward the end of the Iran-Iraq war that so colored the environment in which the Iraqi invasion of Kuwait in August 1990 took place.

In telling irony, it was the American accidental shooting-down of an Iranian airbus in July 1988 by the USS *Vincennes* stationed in the Gulf, killing more than two hundred Iranian passengers, that compelled Ayatollah Khomeini to reluctantly accept UN Security Council Resolution 598 calling for a cease-fire. Khomeini figured that the whole world was against Iran; there were more than one million casualties, and the revolution was petering out—best save what was left before all was lost. Later in July, Khomeini, in what he described as "taking a pill more bitter than poison," accepted Resolution 598. Saddam Hussein, now having the advantage (and foreshadowing characteristics put to more notable use in August 1990), continued to haggle and stall until finally succumbing to international pressure the following month, thus ending the Iran-Iraq war.

In a direct reaction to the Iran-Iraq war, the remaining Gulf states— Saudi Arabia, Kuwait, Bahrain, Qatar, the United Arab Emirates, and Oman—agreed in February 1981 to form the Gulf Cooperation Council (GCC). It was the culmination, in the face of the heightened instability in the region brought about by the Iranian revolution and the Iran-Iraq war, of increasing cooperation among these six Arab Gulf states in previous years, particularly in the area of internal security. The GCC, as originally conceived, was supposed to be more of a security and defense organization than anything else. A number of GCC leaders had called for a joint defense capability that would make the GCC countries as a whole less dependent on external powers, namely the United States. Despite some advances in this sphere, the failure of the GCC to achieve these goals in terms of self-reliant defense became manifest with the Kuwaiti reflagging operation and, most poignantly, the entry of the U.S.-led coalition in 1990–1991 to evict Iraq from Kuwait.

Ironically, the GCC has been most successful in the economic sphere, with the lowering or abolishment of customs duties, the enactment of trade agreements, and the facilitation of freer movement of people and goods within and among the GCC membership.[21] It has also provided a forum for the GCC states to debate and discuss peacefully some of the potentially volatile problems between various members, particularly concerning border demarcation disputes.

In addition, the GCC has allowed Saudi Arabia to play a dominant role within the organization, cementing its new status as a vital player not only in the Persian Gulf area but also in the entire Middle East equation (and forming the triad of powers in the Gulf: Iran, Iraq, and the Saudi-led GCC). Riyadh has used this position to coordinate and unify the often disparate positions of the GCC members when necessary, particularly when the Iran-Iraq war spilled over into GCC territory, mostly in Kuwait.[22] This invariably led to a general tilt toward Iraq in the war, more noticeable with Kuwait, Saudi Arabia, and Bahrain, and less so with Qatar, the UAE, and Oman, the latter three trying to maintain at least cordial relations with Teheran.

Most importantly in the long term, what the formation of the GCC indicated was the beginning of what I call subregional organizations in the Arab world. No longer could the Arab League deal with all of the divergent issues in the Middle East. The Arab world had become too divided as a result of the Egyptian-Israeli peace treaty, the Lebanese civil war (and subsequent Israeli invasion in 1982), and of course, the Iran-Iraq war. In the case of the Iran-Iraq war, the most striking example was the fact that Syria supported non-Arab Iran against Iraq in what at first seemed to be a questionable policy decision on the part of Hafiz al-'Asad. However, considering the long-standing territorial and water-sharing disputes between Iraq and Syria, the ideological and personal hostility between the regimes and leaders, and the chance for Damascus to assert itself in the inter-Arab arena with Egypt on the sidelines and Iraq busy looking in the other direction, it was perfectly logical. The GCC countries felt that their concerns could not be adequately addressed by the Arab League as a whole, given its divided composition; they needed strength in numbers among those who had shared geostrategic and economic interests.

Ironically, as the 1980s wore on, and as the Iran-Iraq war and the Lebanese debacle continued to divide the Arab world, the GCC got stronger, while the Arab League became paralyzed. This was most evident at the November 1987 Arab League summit meeting held in Amman, Jordan, at the behest of the GCC states. The GCC agenda, that is, the Iran-Iraq war, was given priority over other issues. Indeed, it was the first time since the creation of the state of Israel that the Arab-Israeli agenda, namely, the Palestinian issue, was not given top priority. It was also at this summit meeting that the GCC pushed for the re-admittance of Egypt into the Arab fold, for Cairo had been supporting Iraq and Kuwait in the Iran-Iraq war, and its manpower and military capabilities were deemed necessary in order to stem the Iranian tide after 1982. Ironically, Egypt's departure from the Arab fold in 1979 contributed, in my opinion, directly to the Iraqi invasion of Iran, yet it would be that very same war that would rehabilitate Egypt in the Arab world by the late 1980s. The GCC had flexed its muscles, and the Arab League gave way to a subregional grouping. The "balkanization" of the Middle East had begun in earnest in the wake of the failure of Arab nationalism, resulting in a number of Arab states, Egypt, Syria, and the GCC states the most prominent among them, mapping out their own paths. This did not mean that certain countries and subregions became mutually exclusive of each other. Quite the contrary, this evolved into a more integrated matrix, for no area or grouping could be excluded completely from any equation dealing with any significant issue in the region.[23]

The Iraqi invasion of Kuwait in August 1990 and the ensuing Gulf crisis and war for the remainder of that year and into early 1991 represented the next significant repercussion of the Iranian revolution of 1979—through the intervening prism of the Iran-Iraq war. It has often been said that with the invasion of Kuwait, Saddam Hussein was simply taking up where he had left off in 1980 with the invasion of Iran—except that he, and many others, did not expect Iraq to get bogged down in an eight-year conflict. One of the reasons the Arab Gulf states hesitatingly, and sometimes reluctantly, supported Iraq in its war with Iran was the fact that they understood the ambitions of Saddam Hussein, and if he emerged victorious from the war he might turn his irredentist eyes southward toward Kuwait and attempt to dominate the Gulf. It was a prophetic notion. During the Iran-Iraq war, Teheran was the more immediate threat, so the choice of supporting Iraq was clear, in addition to the hope that Baghdad's mending of fences with Washington signaled a more moderate course in the future. But Saddam's obstinacy after Iran accepted UN Resolution 598 in July 1988 as well as his use of chemical weapons against his own people, the Kurds, and the indiscriminate missile attacks against Iranian cities in the latter stages of the war revealed in many people's eyes (but, importantly, not Washington's) the Iraqi president's true colors.

The causes and course of the Gulf crisis and war have been amply delineated elsewhere, so it is not my purpose to rehash well-worn ground.[24] In the region itself, however, the Iraqi invasion of Kuwait and subsequent U.S.-led United Nations response is often referred to as the Second Gulf War, clearly betraying the links with the Iran-Iraq war (or the "first" Gulf war) and the regional instability initiated by the Iranian revolution. These are the connections upon which I will be focusing.

The Iran-Iraq war set the stage for the Iraqi invasion of Kuwait. Iraq's "victory" in its war with Iran was more a matter of Teheran relenting first and accepting the UN cease-fire rather than a result of Iraq's military prowess, although Baghdad did launch a successful counteroffensive in early 1988, retaking the Fao Peninsula, but not without considerable help from the United States and other Western powers. But Saddam Hussein claimed it a victory nonetheless, and therefore he created heightened expectations within the military and among the populace who anticipated some sort of a victory dividend. The problem was that Iraq was severely in debt, having gone from a more than $60 billion surplus before the Iran-Iraq war to a $40 billion debt. As someone once said, dictators need money. Saddam Hussein saw the bank to the south called Kuwait and its lucrative oil fields (which would have given Iraq control of 21 percent of the world's known oil reserves) and wanted to initiate his own type of merger and acquisition. A significant portion of that debt was owed to Kuwait, which, unlike the Saudis, was unwilling to erase it, although the Iraqis argued that they had, in essence, protected Kuwait with their blood and the physical destruction of a good part of Iraq—surely that was worth more than what they owed Kuwait.

In addition, Iraq had some outstanding territorial issues with the Kuwaitis that had not been satisfactorily put to rest, including the Rumaylah oil field that sat astride the border (claiming, apparently accurately, that the Kuwaitis were slant-drilling into the Iraqi side) and the Bubiyan and Warba islands belonging to Kuwait just off its northern coast. The Iranian conquest of the Fao Peninsula had indicated to the Iraqis just how easily they could be cut off from the Gulf—and how crippling this was to its oil industry, and thus its ability to carry out its expansionist designs, especially considering the fact that its overland oil pipelines traversed hostile territory in Syria and Turkey. Iraqi control of the islands would provide it with better access to the Gulf; indeed, the taking of Kuwait itself would expand the Iraqi coastline, thus making it less vulnerable in the future to any Iranian thrust across the Shatt al-Arab waterway, the confluence of the Tigris and Euphrates rivers in southern Iraq that flows into the Persian Gulf.[25]

Perhaps the main reason Saddam Hussein invaded Kuwait is because he thought he could get away with it. In fact, he came very close to it. Why he felt this way also stems from the Iran-Iraq war, particularly the strong strategic and commercial relationship Baghdad built up with the United States during the course of the war, brought together by the mutual desire for preventing an Iranian victory. As mentioned previously, Washington and Baghdad reestablished diplomatic relations in 1984, and the Reagan and Bush administrations believed Iraq could be a very useful surrogate in both the Persian Gulf and Arab-Israeli arenas, filling the empty shoes of both the Shah and Anwar Sadat. Because of this carryover from the previous administration, Bush officials tended to overlook the excesses of Saddam Hussein's actions in the latter part of the war with Iran and in the interim period after the war and preceding the invasion of Kuwait. Indeed, President Bush and his secretary of state, James Baker, admitted in the aftermath of the Gulf war that they "stayed" with Saddam too long, hoping to moderate his policies and to essentially make him into what they wanted. In doing so, they failed to appreciate signals that in fact indicated that he had not changed his colors from 1979–1980: He was an expansionist dictator determined to achieve his national and regional ambitions. Saddam concluded long before Washington did that his ambitions could only be achieved at the cost of his relationship with the United States.[26]

The Iraqi president, on the other hand, in a case of possibly hearing only what he wanted to hear, also failed to read Washington's signals indicating its opposition to his policies, preferring instead the ambiguous statements that U.S. ambassador to Iraq, April Glaspie, and

Assistant Secretary of State for Near Eastern Affairs John Kelly made during the Iraqi military buildup along the Kuwaiti border, which seemed on the surface to portend American disinterest in the affair—as long as the oil continued to flow at reasonable prices, something that Saddam made clear he would do, although the price would rise somewhat from its then glut-induced low level. The U.S. reaction, or apparent lack thereof, tended to confirm to Saddam that at least from the American point of view, the strategic relationship was still alive and thus would hamper, if not totally inhibit, a forceful U.S. response. Baghdad apparently concluded that the United States was still hamstrung by the Vietnam syndrome and that with the end of the superpower cold war (the Iraqi incursion was clearly not directed by Moscow or communist forces, which had been the only occasions since World War II that the United States had sent hundreds of thousands of troops halfway across the world—Korea and Vietnam), Washington had no stomach and little domestic or congressional support for military intervention to protect a nondemocratic regime with which it had not had a particularly close relationship.[27]

Saddam obviously miscalculated. The Bush administration led the charge to liberate Kuwait for a variety of reasons: (1) it did not want Iraq controlling 21 percent of the world's known oil reserves; (2) Iraq had directly threatened Saudi Arabia, an American ally whose borders are the reddest of all red lines in the Middle East—in fact, the decision to move Iraqi troops to the Saudi-Kuwaiti border may have been Saddam Hussein's biggest strategic error;[28] (3) the Bush administration realized as the crisis wore on that it would be a strategic nightmare for the United States to have Iraq's million-man army and weapons-of-mass-destruction capability as a perpetual menace in one of the most vital areas of national interest; (4) unfortunately for Saddam Hussein, President Bush's strategic thinking was not shaped by the Vietnam war syndrome, but by the Munich mentality that emerged out of World War II, in which Bush fought and was decorated. This experience taught Bush and others of this generation not to appease aggressors, as the Europeans had appeased Hitler following his appropriation of the Sudetenland in Czechoslovakia—aggression of this order must not be allowed to stand, and (5) President Bush wanted to implement his New World Order, a new era in the wake of the end of the cold war that would usher in a cooperative international framework to rein in acts of "naked aggression," such as the one perpetrated by Saddam Hussein. Many felt that the United States was exhausted from a half century of cold war and facing what was thought to be the rising economic powers of Europe, led by a united Germany, and East Asia, carried along by the Japanese juggernaut. Many in the administration believed that an assertive response in this situation would reinforce the leadership role of the United States, since it was the only country capable of such a large-scale action.[29]

As is well known, Operation Desert Storm was launched in January 1991 with an intense aerial bombardment campaign and with the ground war commencing in February, a 100-hour thrust that successfully expelled the Iraqis from Kuwait. The (Second) Gulf war was over.

In the aftermath of the war, a *Pax Americana* had been clearly established in the Persian Gulf region, formally (and finally) supplanting the *Pax Britannia* that had enveloped the area for over a century until Britain's evacuation in 1971. From the Nixon Doctrine to the Carter Doctrine to the Kuwaiti reflagging operation, the United States increasingly recognized the value of the Gulf region, and it incrementally enhanced its position in the Persian Gulf zone until the climactic interlude of 1990–1991 inserted American might straight into the mix. It spelled the end of balance-of-power politics; the United States would no longer rely on either Iran or Iraq to be its gendarme in the Persian Gulf. Instead defense cooperation agreements were consummated between Washington and most of the GCC countries (Saudi Arabia did not formally sign since it already had an intimate strategic defense relationship with the United States) and equipment and materiel were prepositioned just in case military action again became necessary—for although defeated, Saddam remained in power.

Because the GCC had already shown it was incapable of providing for its own defense, the United States adopted a forward policy in the region that required a significant direct presence. The flip side of this new strategic environment was the "dual containment" of Iraq and Iran. The term "containment," of course, was quite popular in the early 1990s, since the policy it described was deemed successful in winning the cold war with the Soviet Union. Why not apply it at the regional level in the Persian Gulf against two so-called rogue countries? It was hoped that containment, through economic, political, and military pressure, would compel a change of regime-type, if not ideology, toward a more compliant, cooperative, and internationally acceptable status.

Although dual containment has come under intense scrutiny, and even criticism, in recent years, especially as a more moderate regime came to power in Teheran in the form of Muhammad Khatami's stunning presidential victory in 1997 and as the cat-and-mouse game with Saddam Hussein has continued over the extent of Iraq's compliance with post-Gulf war UN resolutions, the enhanced American presence in the region has remained, often producing a negative backlash among the Gulf Arab populations who had before the Gulf war become accustomed to, at best, a detached relationship with the United States.[30] This backlash has become more pronounced in recent years as the UN sanctions against Iraq, kept in place largely through the determined efforts of Washington, are increasingly seen in the Gulf and elsewhere as unnecessarily punitive and political, hurting only the Iraqi people rather than undermining the regime of Saddam Hussein. Even during the Gulf crisis, when the United Nations coalition was building up its forces in the region, there were rumblings in the Muslim world regarding the presence of "infidels" in Saudi Arabia, the site of Islam's two holiest sites—Mecca and Medina. In fact, it was this perceived affront that initiated Osama bin Laden's quest against the United States. What was at first a call to remove all foreign troops from Saudi Arabia and bring down what bin Laden viewed as a corrupt, subservient, and un-Islamic Saudi regime later grew into a transnational terrorist network expounding a global jihad against the United States, Israel, and their allies. Indeed, it has evolved into a jihad against all identified godless and infidel regimes that repress Muslims, as evidenced by bin Laden's apparent involvement in areas as diverse as the Chechnyan separatist movement against Russia, the Muslim Uighurs in the Xinjiang province of China, and the Moros in the Philippines.

Despite this negative backlash, the Gulf war had a salutary effect upon the Arab-Israeli arena. When the Bush administration began to meticulously piece together the UN coalition against Iraq, it was expected that the Gulf Arab states as well as Washington's traditional allies in the Arab world, Egypt and Morocco, would join up. With the

end of the cold war and the Soviet Union desperately needing economic assistance from the West, it was also not surprising that
Moscow, and even Beijing, supported the coalition by not utilizing
their vetoes in the UN Security Council. Saddam Hussein's flouting of
international norms and the reported atrocities perpetrated inside
Kuwait made it difficult for any country to come out openly against
the U.S.-led multinational force. The participation of Syria, however,
was most important of all the Arab states in the coalition, and it was
this participation that prepared the foundation for the postwar Madrid
peace process. Syria's inclusion made it seem like it was almost the
entire Arab world against Iraq rather than the usual pro-West suspects,
especially since Damascus had been the vanguard of the anti-Israeli
front for decades.[31]

Even though Israel was not a member of the coalition, despite
Saddam Hussein's attempts to draw it into the fray by lobbing SCUD
missiles into Israeli proper, hoping to turn a Persian Gulf conflict into
an Arab-Israeli one, the Arab states in the coalition and Tel Aviv were
de facto on the same side in the war, with similar objectives. This
political and strategic reorganization and, maybe most importantly,
the broken psychological barriers—combined, of course, with the decisive coalition victory—altered the regional balance of power, with
Washington as the clear dominant outside force. The comprehensive
peace process launched at Madrid in October 1991, cosponsored by the
United States and the Soviet Union, was the natural outcome.

Even though the Madrid meeting initiated an oftentimes halting
process that on several occasions made more progress in its tangential
application than in the proscribed pathways, it was the first time that
Israel and the bordering Arab states (still officially at war with Israel)
met publicly face to face. The Israeli-PLO accords signed on the White
House lawn in September 1993, although negotiated for the most part
outside of the Madrid process, and the Israeli-Jordanian peace treaty of
1994 both owe their consummations to the repercussions of the Gulf
war. An Israeli-Syrian peace process also began as a result of the
Madrid meeting that at times came very close to fruition (particularly
in early 1996 and in late 1999-early 2000). Although negotiations were
broken off in spring 2000, the strategic choice for peace, including a
return of the Golan Heights to Syria, was made by both sides.

The Egyptian-Israeli Peace Treaty

A sine qua non of Arab strategy and hope for successfully confronting Israel for three decades prior to 1979 was the active leadership of Egypt, traditionally the most populous and militarily the strongest state in the Arab world. Without Egypt, the Arab states could not hope to defeat Israel in battle, and various countries and groups would be resigned to a strategy of pinpricking the Jewish state and/or adopting a defensive deterrent posture. Not uncoincidentally, it had been one of the primary objectives of a succession of Israeli (and American) leaders to somehow pry Egypt apart from the rest of the Arab world, isolating it and drawing it into an alliance with the West. Egypt had been a relative newcomer to the Arab nationalist front anyway; it was a country that had its own proud heritage and saw itself straddling North Africa and Southwest Asia. If Tel Aviv could somehow engineer this, then the permanency of the Jewish state would be undeniable—and its ability to counter any other Arab threat, either from an individual state or a coalition of states, would be unquestioned.

In essence, the 1979 Egyptian-Israeli peace treaty ended the Arab-Israeli conflict in its original form; that is, there would be no more coalitions of Arab states attempting to defeat Israel. An all-out regional conflict characteristic of the 1967 and 1973 Arab-Israeli wars was a moot point in the foreseeable future—or as long as Israel and Egypt remained on relatively good terms. From the Arab perspective, achieving the full and just rights of the Palestinians became infinitely more difficult the moment Anwar Sadat signed along the dotted line—the Arab world had just lost most of its leverage.

The removal of Egypt from the Arab fold created a vacuum of power in the Arab world and significantly disturbed the regional order. Instantly, the vulnerability of Arab countries such as Syria and Iraq was, in their view, heightened considerably, and the Israeli regime of Prime Minister Menachim Begin began to think that it could act aggressively on a number of fronts with impunity. It was not a surprise that Syria and Iraq, both ruled officially by the socialist Ba'th party, cooperated for a short time following the signing of the peace treaty in an attempt to present a united front against Israel. The Iraqi-Syrian entente would break apart shortly thereafter because of the inherent differences and territorial squabbles between the two countries. The respective regimes emerged from rival branches of the Ba'th party and water-sharing issues concerning the downstream riparian status of the Euphrates River remained a nagging sore between Damascus and Baghdad. In addition, historically in the post–World War II period, whenever Egypt decided to follow its own course based on nationalistic interest rather than pan-Arab unity, Iraq and/or Syria would attempt to fill the perceived void and vault into the leadership position within the Arab world. Indeed, the Arab cold war in the late 1950s and throughout much of the 1960s was based largely on the inter-Arab rivalry between this triad of powers.[32]

With Egypt on the sidelines after abandoning its traditional leadership role, both Syria and Iraq would desperately try to fill its shoes— and this could not be done together. The rivalry between Damascus and Baghdad, subsumed to a large degree until 1979, would come out into the open after the peace treaty, affecting inter-Arab relationships and alliances to the present day and shaping the tremendously important decisions by Syrian President Hafiz al-'Asad to support Iran against Iraq in the Iran-Iraq war and to support the UN coalition against Iraq in 1990–1991. Ironically, it would be the latter Syrian decision that was so significant in formulating the Madrid peace process, one that in many ways took its cue from the Egyptian-Israeli example. In fact, with Iraq's understandable preoccupation with matters to its east, Egypt's isolation within the Arab world, brought about by the peace treaty, immediately thrust Syria into the limelight in the confrontation with Israel. It also compelled the Soviet Union to deepen its relationship with Damascus: "Assad would henceforth be adopted by both the USSR and the Arab mainstream as the undisputed leader of the struggle against Israel. This regional and international consecration had substantial legitimizing effects on this minority-led regime."[33]

With Egypt out of the picture for the time being, the Arab world began to disintegrate into regional blocs, whether willingly or unwillingly. As Ghassan Salame writes, "A North African (maghribi) or a Gulf Arab (khaliji) identity, which had once been an anathema, was no longer so, and the 'Egypt first' slogan that had once been held in check gradually became acceptable." He continues by stating,

The geographical disintegration of the regional system into local subsystems also had a legitimizing ideology but not a vocal one. Subsystems
were ostensibly founded on realism, which is an ideology in itself. In fact,
this ideology's discourse was produced after these internally integrated but
loosely connected local subsystems were established. More often than not,
local groupings were formed around a newly assertive local power.[34]

Saudi Arabia took the lead in forming the GCC not only because of
the Iranian revolution and subsequent Iran-Iraq war but also because
Egypt was no longer there as a partner, protector, or patron in the inter-
Arab arena. The GCC could better represent Saudi and Gulf Arab
interests than an Arab League bereft of the moderating and unifying
influence of Egypt. Syria, with its self-anointed role as the last stand
against Israeli expansionism and hegemony, began its trek to dominate
the politics of the Levant, including Lebanon, Jordan, and the PLO. It
would begin a very complicated political matrix with regard to peace
plans and negotiations, and it seemed throughout the 1980s Jordan and
the PLO were looking over their shoulders at the Syrian response to
any moves they made toward negotiations with Israel over the
Palestinian problem as a result of intense pressure from the United
States and moderate Arab states. With intervening events, such as the
1982 Israeli invasion of Lebanon, the end of the superpower cold war,
and the 1990–1991 Gulf crisis and war, Syria would emerge victorious
in Lebanon, but the PLO and Jordan would eventually tread their own
paths toward peace, as evidenced by the 1993 Israeli-PLO accords and
the 1994 Jordanian-Israeli peace treaty.

Two countries, or at least the regimes ruling them, seemed to be
emboldened by Egypt's departure from the active playing field in the
Middle East: Iraq and Israel. Subsequent actions by each, unfortunately, would have devastating results.

Iraq's situation in the wake of the Egyptian-Israeli peace treaty has
largely been discussed earlier in this chapter. As stated, the fact that
the two emergency Arab League summit meetings convened in reaction to both the Camp David accords in September 1978 and the
signing of the treaty in March 1979 were held in Baghdad symbolized the new inter-Arab future Saddam Hussein hoped to mold.[35] On
October 30, 1979, Iraq renounced the 1975 Algiers Agreement with
Iran, by which Iran pledged to curtail its support of Kurds in Iraq in

return for concessions on determining the border along the Shatt al-Arab waterway. The agreement had, at least for a few years, ameliorated tensions between Baghdad and Teheran; its renunciation certainly indicated the more bellicose direction in which Saddam was headed. His pan-Arab charter enunciated in early 1980 supplied further evidence of his self-anointed leadership role within the Arab world. With the effective removal of Egypt from the Arab equation, there was no brake on Iraq's attempts to achieve its dual ambitions of obtaining a hegemonic position in both the Arab-Israeli and Persian Gulf arenas.

Even if Egypt had not signed the treaty with Israel and had remained an active player in inter-Arab politics and diplomacy, Saddam Hussein's quest for power may still have gone unchecked. But without Cairo's moderating influence (which may have been less aligned with Washington's objectives had it not signed the treaty and officially continued the state of war with Israel), the opportunity to take advantage of the apparent post-revolution chaos in Iran and to expand his power base in the region was that much more enticing. And Egypt, rather than utilizing the Iran-Iraq war, as it dragged on and on and Iraq's position became more and more vulnerable, to rebuild its Arab credentials and reenter the Arab fold by sending thousands of "volunteers" to defend Arab Iraq from non-Arab Iran, might have been able to play a different role in relation to the war, one that could have evolved into a constructive mediating position that might have contained Baghdad and shortened the conflict. Of course, these are all hypothetical "what if's."

On the other hand, benefits derived from Egypt's continuing leadership role in the Persian Gulf arena might have been offset by the still festering Arab-Israeli conflict. The 1973 Arab-Israeli war demonstrated the escalatory nature of the conflict, having come close to a superpower nuclear confrontation in its waning moments. Fear of what another conflict might look like in the wake of this close call was a significant part of the motivation of all the parties involved to let the air out of the expanding balloon of military destructiveness. The Iran-Iraq war remained relatively contained, even though the final results of the war laid the foundation for Iraq's 1990 invasion of Kuwait. But the thought of another all-out Arab-Israeli conflict, just when the superpower cold war was heating up again in the late 1970s and early

1980s, sent shudders down the spines of anyone who feared the classic case of a regional conflagration escalating to a superpower standoff, not to mention what would surely be catastrophic repercussions for the parties directly involved in battle in the region itself.

The Lebanese, however, might disagree with any analysis that implied that the Egyptian-Israeli peace treaty, while severely flawed and disruptive, was overall a positive event simply because it prevented a cataclysm. For Lebanon, the cataclysm came just the same.

Predictions of doom and gloom by the many critics of the Egyptian-Israeli peace treaty were, at least in their eyes, proven true: Israel became much more aggressive. In 1981 Israel bombed a suspected nuclear reactor in Iraq, extended Israeli law over (de facto annexing) the Golan Heights, and accelerated the building of Jewish settlements in the remaining occupied territories, primarily in the West Bank. But it was the 1982 Israeli invasion of Lebanon that clinched the case. As with the other significant events described in this book, the Israeli invasion has been examined ad nauseam. Critics of Israeli policy, particularly those arraigned against the right-wing Likud regime of Menachem Begin, contend that the removal of Egypt from the Arab battle plan allowed Israel to pursue its interests vis-à-vis its northern neighbors, since the southern flank had been secured through peace. Whether this was a specific intention of the Egyptian-Israeli peace treaty is another matter. But surely the Israelis knew the isolation of Egypt would significantly weaken the Arab world as a whole. The PLO, now operating out of Lebanon and feeling left out in the cold by Sadat's separate peace, intensified their guerrilla operations against Israel in order to, at the very least, block any sort of emerging Arab moderate consensus that Sadat and the United States had half-heartedly been trying to generate toward a comprehensive peace accord— operations that were supported vigorously by countries such as Syria and Iraq.

To say that there was no provocation from Lebanese soil would misrepresent the situation. The Israelis had invaded southern Lebanon in 1978 in an attempt to clear out PLO positions that had been threatening northern Israeli settlements. However, the question is whether the operation in 1982, the extent of which would become known in short order, greatly exceeded the actual threat. The "hidden agenda" of

Begin and his defense minister, Ariel Sharon, quickly answers the preceding question in the affirmative, laying the groundwork for what many have called Israel's biggest foreign policy mistake. Already reeling from years of civil war, Lebanon would experience more destruction, ruin, divisiveness, and pain, and a generation would be further lost in the agony of a Middle East battleground.

What was anticipated as a sweep of PLO positions in south Lebanon, à la 1978, soon devolved into the Israeli government's ultimate goal: the removal of the PLO (and hopefully Syria) entirely from Lebanon and the placement of a Lebanese Maronite Christian ally as president who would sign a peace treaty with Israel.[36] Begin and Sharon were playing kingmaker, a purely offensive role that was uncharacteristic of the Israelis. That is, all of the major wars involving Israel up to that point, while taking preemptive action on a number of occasions, were all logically rationalized as necessary for the survival of the state. This was different, and most Israelis, especially as the Lebanese quagmire became evident, vehemently opposed this type of great power imperialism.

The PLO was prepared to fight to the last before being escorted out of Beirut (and into effective exile in Tunis) by a multinational force led by the United States. The Syrians would also fight back, in the process usually being obliterated when directly confronting the Israelis. But Damascus would adjust and adopt more covert and, as it turned out, more effective measures against both the Israelis and the Western multinational force that increasingly became identified as simply a support system to achieve through international peacekeeping and diplomacy what the Israelis could not accomplish through brute force.[37] In October 1983, 241 U.S. marines and scores of other Western military personnel, officials, and civilians paid for this change of tactics with their lives. The chaotic repercussions of the Israeli invasion and occupation, the subsequent withdrawal of the multinational force in February 1984 (and having been burned in Lebanon, the Reagan Administration, until the last year of its tenure in power, essentially withdrew from Middle Eastern affairs and focused on its obsession with the Soviet Union), and the retreat by Israel further south in 1985 fueled the fractiousness of Lebanese religio-political society that was already an ideal receptor to external interference. As long as Lebanon remained relatively aloof from the Arab-Israeli conflict, compromises could be arranged and the inherent divisiveness could be papered over. But events in the 1970s, beginning with the relocation of the PLO to Beirut after being expelled from Jordan in 1970, capped off with the Israeli invasion in 1982, invariably entangled what had been a peaceful and prosperous nation into conflict at all levels. Soon enough Lebanon became a proxy for almost every conceivable dispute in the area. The Iran-Iraq war, the Arab-Israeli conflict, and to a lesser extent, the superpower cold war would all be fought simultaneously in Lebanon. Implosion and destruction would be the natural results.

Some of the more infamous repercussions of the Israeli invasion have already been discussed, such as the Iran-Contra affair, the radicalization of the Shiite community in Lebanon that created an opening for the entrance of Iranian influence and the creation of Hizbullah, and the subordination of the country to Syria, which after all was said and done, emerged as the victor and power broker. This was in no small part due to the decision by the Gulf war allies to essentially "give" Lebanon to Damascus as the quid pro quo for the latter's participation in the coalition against Iraq. Having been so squarely attached to Syria, the Lebanese situation has become even more a function of the Israeli-Syrian equation and negotiations. Hafiz al-'Asad saw Hizbullah as a necessary lever against Israel in Lebanon that could be traded in for a full Israeli withdrawal from the Golan Heights. The unilateral Israeli withdrawal from its security zone in south Lebanon in May 2000 has removed this lever for the time being from the Syrian basket, but it is still unclear as of this writing whether this has effectively restored Lebanon's desired aloofness from the Arab-Israeli conflict. A new president in Damascus, moderate forces improving their position in Teheran (and the apparent urging of Hizbullah to rein in its military activity against Israel and develop its political role in Lebanon following the Israeli withdrawal), and Hizbullah's own enhanced popularity and legitimacy in Lebanon in the wake of its success in forcing Israel to retreat (in effect, being the first Arab contingent to defeat Israel) still leave many questions unanswered as to the relationship between the Jewish state and its multifarious neighbor to the north, and indeed, the overall future of Lebanon itself.

There has been a great deal of criticism aimed at the Egyptian-Israeli peace treaty over the years, much of which has revolved around the disruptive aftereffects just discussed: the 1982 Israeli invasion of Lebanon and the Iran-Iraq war. But it has also been criticized—or more to the point, Anwar Sadat has been vilified in the Arab world—for essentially abandoning the Palestinian cause. The Camp David accords were composed of two frameworks for peace, one of which dealt with Egyptian-Israeli bilateral issues such as the return of the Sinai Peninsula, security measures, and normalization, and the other of which dealt with progress toward a comprehensive agreement, including the Palestinian issue. The major flaw in the accords was the fact that the two frameworks were not linked; that is, progress on the Egyptian-Israeli framework did not necessarily have to be matched by progress on the Palestinian issue. So while Begin and Sadat hurried to consummate the one, the other tended to languish and/or be ignored. The Israeli prime minister was in the strongest negotiating position at Camp David, unlike Sadat and President Carter, who both went far out on the proverbial limb and had to show something coming out of the Maryland presidential retreat—a mediocre deal was better than no deal at all. Begin, on the other hand, was in the catbird seat. He and his regime would survive intact regardless of whether a deal was had, and on at least the issue of linking the Egyptian-Israeli framework with an overall Arab-Israeli peace, he could sit back and wait for his demands to be met and for Sadat to make most of the concessions. Sadat at least wanted to make sure that he did not give the outward appearance that he had downgraded the priority of the Palestinian issue; that is, he wanted cover. And although he would attempt to revive the Palestinian issue with Israel after the signing of the treaty, a truculent Begin was not about to negotiate away any more land. In his own mind and in those of his supporters, Resolution 242 had been met and territories (and not "the" territories) had been returned; now his regime could go about consolidating Israel's position on the remainder of the occupied territories, especially the West Bank, with a systematic acceleration of building and expanding Jewish settlements. So although the chances of a regional conflagration lessened as a result of the treaty, Palestinian frustration increased, combining with the PLO's predicament in Lebanon to produce the fury of the *intifada* by the late

1980s. As was Begin's intent, more Israeli settlements in the occupied territories made it that much more difficult to trade any more of the "Land of Israel" for peace with the Palestinians or Israel's Arab neighbors. The Egyptian-Israeli peace treaty, in the minds of many Israelis, certainly more within Likud than Labor, let the air out of the balloon of pressure building on the Jewish state to relinquish occupied territory in accordance with UN resolutions. The return of the Sinai bought time, and the distraction of the Israeli invasion of Lebanon and the divisiveness in the Arab world brought about by the Iran-Iraq war also bought time. The delay, however, produced the complicated and tortuous negotiations between successive Israeli leaders and the PLO (PNA) since the signing of the Israeli-PLO accords in 1993.

On the other hand, the Egyptian-Israeli peace treaty has lasted, despite many serious bumps on the road, particularly the Israeli invasion of Lebanon, which almost ruptured the relationship. Normalization of relations between the two countries has not occurred, certainly not anywhere near the extent many had hoped for when the treaty was signed. At times it seems the only element maintaining the peace is the close (some would say bounded) relationship each country has with the United States. The fact that Jordan signed a peace treaty with Israel in 1994, only a year after the Israeli-PLO accords, along with a plethora of other Arab nations that have de facto, if not de jure, established relations with Israel at a variety of levels, lessened the perceived isolation within the Arab world that many Egyptians felt in being the only Arab nation to make peace with Israel for fifteen years. Indeed, Egypt became a major partner of the United States in Washington's quest to broker peace agreements between Israel and the remainder of its Arab neighbors; in a sense, Cairo was assuming its traditional leadership position in the Arab world, although this time around in a much different fashion than in the Nasserist era. But tension between Egypt and Israel, and more specifically between Egyptians and Israelis, has remained, and to some degree it has even grown in recent years as frustration over lack of progress on the Palestinian and Syrian peace fronts have led to further disillusionment in Arab quarters and as Cairo and Tel Aviv increasingly see each other, politically and economically, as regional rivals.[38]

However, the peace treaty has somehow survived. And by doing so, it has, despite its acknowledged flaws, provided something of a template for succeeding Arab-Israeli agreements and destroyed psychological barriers. This last point may be the most important long-term development. As Saad Eddin Ibrahim states:

> Most Egyptians may be disenchanted, disillusioned, or outraged at Israeli behavior. Some organized political forces have continuously called for the abrogation of Camp David and the treaty, and several have called for the severing of relations and an end to normalization. But none has reiterated the pre-1977 language of existential negation. None has suggested a declaration of war or a return to the state of war with the Jewish state. Camp David "normalized the feelings" of most Egyptians toward Israel across the spectrum—hate, anger, disapproval, acceptance, accommodation, and even disposition for cooperation—but no negation.[39]

The Egyptian-Israeli peace treaty has had enormous influence at a practical level as well. The ideas of phased withdrawals, interim agreements, and secluded settings for negotiations among the respective leaders, such as Camp David and the Wye Plantation, have all found their way into the lexicon and process of peace; the "modalities" of peace often became as important as the prospective peace agreement itself. Security arrangements, border demarcations, and early warning systems are all a part of the discussion in recent and current Middle East peace negotiations; all of these items owe a significant part of their origins to the Egyptian-Israeli peace treaty and the process that led up to it. In addition, the role of the United States in Middle East peace negotiations was inestimably enhanced. It became clear that Washington was the only power able to extract even the tiniest of concessions from Israel. Its role as a broker at some level in future Arab-Israeli negotiations, which today is somewhat taken for granted, became formalized with the treaty. As Quandt writes,

> Whatever one thought of the contents of the Camp David Accords, all saw that the United States had played an essential part. On his own, Sadat would probably have gotten far less from Israel, and indeed it is questionable whether a deal could have been struck at all. This realiza-

tion raised the question of whether or not the United States could be brought back into the game to do for the Palestinians—and perhaps the Syrians as well—what it had done for Sadat.[40]

It is, of course, no coincidence that PLO Chairman Yasir Arafat and Israeli Prime Minister Ehud Barak were summoned by President Clinton to Camp David in July 2000 in a last-ditch effort to settle the troublesome final status issues before the Clinton administration left office.[41] Even some of the events within the 1978 version were symbolically replicated in the 2000 version, such as a visit by the respective delegations to nearby Gettysburg, obviously meant as an implicit message to avoid the carnage of the American civil war, and the "suitcase" diplomacy, whereby delegations would overtly make arrangements to abruptly leave the meetings, thereby inducing a crisis atmosphere that would hopefully jump-start stagnant talks to another level. Clinton officials were obviously hoping to recreate some of the magic of September 1978.

The Egyptian-Israeli peace process has even negatively affected, to some degree, the current status of Arab-Israeli negotiations. One of the reasons Syria's President Hafiz al-'Asad and, apparently, his successor son, Bashar, have doggedly insisted on a return of the entire Golan Heights to the June 4, 1967 line (restoring the pre–1967 war boundaries) is their desire to get back more land than Sadat retrieved through the 1979 peace treaty, a treaty that, as discussed previously, 'Asad vehemently rejected. In the Sinai, the 1923 international border drawn by the British mandatory power between Egypt and then Palestine was the border established between Israel and Egypt in 1979 (and actually put into effect when the last portion of the Sinai was returned in April 1982). The 1923 international border drawn by the British and French mandatory power between Syria and then Palestine is some 10 meters off of the Sea of Galilee in the northeastern portion of the area bordering the southern portion of the Golan Heights. This was, of course, purposely done by the British to keep the French away from this important water source that today provides approximately 30 percent of Israel's water needs. The June 4, 1967, line represents Syrian advances to the Sea of Galilee acquired in the 1947–1949 Arab-Israeli war and through sporadic fighting with Israel in the years between the creation of Israel in 1948 and the 1967 war. The importance of this small sliver of territory is more symbolic than anything else, but Syrian leaders have repeatedly stated publicly that they are absolutely committed to accepting nothing less than this. In this way, at least Syrians can point to the fact that holding out for a much longer period of time than Egypt netted a bit more in return.

One could also speculate that Arafat's intransigence at the Camp David negotiations in July 2000 was, in part, due to the overwhelming perception in the Arab world that Sadat gave up too much in 1978.[42] Since Sadat had already relinquished his main bargaining chip by traveling to Israel in 1977 and clearly committed himself to a peaceful settlement, he felt compelled to come away from Camp David with an Israeli commitment to return the entire Sinai. Sadat was, therefore, in a weak bargaining position, and he was subsequently pressured by the Americans to make the most concessions. One sensed a great deal of apprehension in the Arab world over whether Camp David 2000 would be a repeat of Camp David 1978, only this time with the Palestinians. One must remember that the 1978 Camp David accords and 1979 peace treaty are not viewed nearly as positively in the Arab world as they are in the United States and Israel. There was no "magic" in the Catoctin Mountains of Maryland; indeed, most Arabs called the treaty a capitulation and heretical abandonment. Arafat did not want to repeat the perceived mistakes of Sadat.

In a way, Arafat's position during the meeting in Maryland, which was based on the exhortations of the PLO chairman's constituency in the occupied territories, was more akin to Begin's in 1978–1979; that is, he would be vilified if he signed onto a deal that conceded too much. In other words, he would win if he settled the final status issues in the Palestinian favor, and he would win if he was perceived to be standing fast in the face of Israeli and American pressure and not giving in on those issues that are sacred to the Palestinian cause, such as Jerusalem and the return of Palestinian refugees. Sadat paid for the peace treaty with his life; Arafat wanted to make sure the same did not happen to him.

The Soviet Invasion of Afghanistan

Though at first somewhat peripheral to the Middle East, the Soviet invasion of Afghanistan may have had the most influential global repercussions of all of the significant events of 1979. Not only was change brought about in the Middle East, which would become more and more evident as time passed, but the domestic fronts in both the Soviet Union and the United States were dramatically affected (not to speak of the utter destruction of the country of Afghanistan). And when the two superpowers are so dramatically affected, perforce, the rest of the world also experiences the repercussions.

Moscow's involvement in Afghanistan became known as the Soviet Union's "Vietnam," and it lasted until the Geneva Accords were signed in April 1988, with the last Soviet troops exiting in February 1989.[43] It was a war that grew more and more unpopular with the Soviet public as it dragged on year after year, with the growing unlikelihood of any real chance of a conclusive victory.[44] Even though the Soviets lost "only" about a quarter of the number of soldiers (13,000–15,000) that the United States lost in Vietnam, the social and economic drain was readily apparent. The Soviet economy, already reeling from typical socialist inefficiency, corruption, and statist intrusion, could ill afford the quagmire that Afghanistan became. In a very real sense, the Soviet Union's entanglement in Afghanistan was the last straw for the Soviet system. It was the penultimate chapter of Soviet communism, overloading the system toward implosion— George Kennan was finally proven correct. In response to American pressure against Soviet activities in Third World cold war hot spots, such as Central America, Africa, and the Middle East, a new generation of Soviet leaders, feeling little if any responsibility for the Afghani mistake, chief among them Soviet Premier Mikhail Gorbachev, decided that rather than try to keep up with the United States in maintaining the superpower standoff, they would just end the cold war. With the end of the cold war also, not surprisingly, came the end of the Soviet Union—in effect the Soviet empire—by late 1991.

The experience of Afghanistan also had a sobering effect upon Soviet foreign policy ideology, which has continued to have reverberations in the new Russia. Many of the assumptions of the Stalin/Khrushchev/

Brezhnev eras regarding the socialist transformation of Third World countries were reevaluated (or encountered a more critical audience), which became a crucial formative element in Gorbachev's "new political thinking." Many Soviet academics and policymakers had for a number of years suggested "that quite specific conditions might be necessary for a country to jump successfully from a feudal or pre-feudal society to socialism, bypassing capitalism. They argued the importance of the cultural and structural peculiarities of particular countries, and they warned against 'leftist' miscalculations that could lead to debacles."[45] With the Afghanistan episode fulfilling this prophecy, Moscow perforce became much more cautious in terms of Third World intervention. Foreign policy became a much more practical affair; in essence, the Soviet Union's foreign policy paradigm progressed through a stage of what Georgiy Mirsky calls "de-ideologization."[46] As Richard Falk states:

> Soviet withdrawal from Afghanistan is consistent with the overall thrust of Gorbachev's leadership as embodied especially in the proceedings of the historic 27th Congress of the Soviet Communist Party—namely, according priority to *perestroika* [i.e., domestic reform]; reducing East-West tensions; and eliminating by unilateral initiative expensive and unsuccessful Soviet commitments overseas, especially in the Third World . . . and to take account of an intense, if provisional, process of internal self-criticism that repudiates virtually all aspects of Brezhnev era foreign policy.[47]

With economic necessity and practicality driving foreign policy in the late 1980s and early 1990s, the Soviet Union/Russia, in cooperation with the West, supported diplomatic resolutions to a host of conflicts, such as in the Iran-Iraq war, Namibia, and Angola; even the United Nations was entrusted by Moscow with a central role in these and other diplomatic settlements.[48] The fruition of this transformation was, of course, the Kremlin's support, even if somewhat passive, of the UN-mandated Gulf war coalition to evict from Kuwait a country that had signed a Treaty of Friendship and Cooperation with Moscow and had had a long economic and military relationship with the Soviet Union as one of the bastions of socialist-style Third World development.

Both the Soviet invasion of and withdrawal from Afghanistan had at least tangential influence on the perception of the Soviet Union by a variety of quarters, which may have affected policy decisions. For instance, some have suggested that the Soviet entrenchment in the Afghani mess emboldened opposition movements in Eastern European countries, particularly in Poland; it was felt the Soviets would not be able, in fact would not dare, to launch a Czech-like operation of military suppression while entangled in the mountains, valleys, and ravines around Kabul and Herat. Certainly the repercussions of Afghanistan and the new political thinking loosened the Soviet embrace of Eastern Europe toward the symbolic end of its dominance with the fall of the Berlin Wall in 1989. In addition, it is possible that the Reagan administration may have been encouraged to intervene against leftist regimes and groups in Central America (and elsewhere) not only because of what was perceived to be an enhanced Soviet threat as demonstrated by its actions in Central Asia but also because it too possibly believed that the Soviets would be less able to fight the cold war globally while ensconced in Afghanistan.[49]

The flip side of this supposition is that leftist regimes and groups ascertained from the Soviet withdrawal from Afghanistan that the days of earnest political, military, and economic support from Moscow were over; therefore, alternative paths toward resolution of their respective situations had to be more seriously considered, especially diplomatic solutions rather than military ones. In the Middle East, this resulted in countries, such as Syria, and groups, such as the PLO, feeling compelled to moderate their positions vis-à-vis the Arab-Israeli conflict and the United States, as they were now basically bereft of energetic Soviet support. This, in combination with the post-Gulf war environment in the region, laid the foundation for the Madrid peace process and the ongoing Arab-Israeli negotiations.

In the short term, however, Moscow's gambit in Afghanistan backfired on its position in the Middle East, something the Kremlin obviously considered but felt was worth the risk. The Soviet leadership possibly did not envision how deleterious the invasion was to become for the U.S.S.R. in the region. As Robert O. Freedman states:

At the time of the invasion, the Arab world was basically united in opposing the U.S.-supported Camp David accords, and, except for its ties with
Egypt and Israel, the U.S. position in the Middle East was a weak one.
Pro-Soviet regimes had emerged in Ethiopia and South Yemen, America's
ally, the Shah of Iran, had fallen, to be replaced by the virulently anti-
American Khomeini regime that was holding American diplomats
hostage, and even in Arab countries that had once been close to the
United States, such as Saudi Arabia and Jordan, there were deep misgiv-
ings about the nature and steadfastness of U.S. policy in the Middle East.
Given the fact that Moscow had looked upon the Arab world as a region
of zero-sum game influence competition with the United States, it
appeared clear that the Soviet Union was winning, and the United States
was losing the influence competition.[50]

For Moscow's position in the Middle East, the invasion was terribly
bad timing, just as most of the Arab world was uniting behind it in the
post–Egyptian-Israeli peace treaty environment, symbolized by the formation of the Steadfastness Front—a league of Arab states opposed to
the peace process. The invasion was something that most Arab states
were compelled to oppose on grounds of Muslim solidarity and/or
anti-imperialism. Even though Steadfastness Front states such as
Syria, Libya, and South Yemen cautiously supported the invasion,
other members such as the PLO and Algeria questioned Moscow's
actions.[51] And a possible opportunity to make some inroads in Iran,
now that it was thoroughly at odds with the United States, crumbled,
as the new Islamic republic also was compelled to vehemently oppose
the invasion. In addition, as will be described in more detail below, the
move into Afghanistan awakened the United States from its post-
Vietnam slumber, refocusing Washington's radar screen to the Persian
Gulf, which led to a systematic buildup of U.S. power in the region,
exactly what the Soviets were hoping to avoid.[52]

Ironically, although the Afghani imbroglio accelerated the breakup
of the Soviet Union and helped bring an end to the cold war, it was this
very Soviet intervention that for one last gasp reignited the cold war
and led to dramatic changes in the direction of American politics.

As mentioned in Chapter 2, the United States was caught somewhat
unaware regarding Soviet intentions in Afghanistan until it was much

too late to do anything that might forestall the invasion. The perceived passivity of the Carter administration regarding the Iranian revolution as well as the hostage crisis might well have emboldened Kremlin leaders to sanction the invasion, the fear of a strong American response having been relatively downgraded as a result. To many in Moscow, the détente that had defined the U.S.-Soviet relationship in the early 1970s had been unraveling for several years, and the Carter administration's establishment of full diplomatic relations with the People's Republic of China earlier in January 1979 heightened the threat to the Soviet Union and contributed mightily to its perceived isolation. Therefore, security concerns, not diplomatic ones, seemed to move to the forefront, and if a withering détente became a victim, so be it.[53]

The Carter administration reacted strongly to the Soviet invasion, and the president became a belated cold warrior. Fearing that the Soviet action could be a prelude toward establishing a hegemonic position in Gulf (the invasion theoretically put the Soviets only 500 kilometers from the Arabian Sea), taking advantage of the fall of the Shah and subsequent American exit from Iran, the president announced in January 1980 what came to be known as the Carter Doctrine. The Soviet invasion was viewed by Carter administration officials not as a defensive action meant to create a *cordon sanitaire* along its southern belly, much like Eastern Europe on the Soviet Union's eastern flank, but as an aggressive offensive move toward the Persian Gulf and Indian Ocean, in line with the old Czarist Russian model.[54] In Carter's State of the Union address on January 23, 1980, outlining the Carter Doctrine, he stated the following: "Any attempt by any outside force to gain control of the Persian Gulf region will be regarded as an assault on the vital interests of the United States of America, and such an assault will be repelled by any means necessary, including military force."[55] As Gary Sick has pointed out, this enunciation was quite similar to the "classic" statement by Lord Lansdowne in 1903 describing British policy toward the Gulf in which he said that the United Kingdom would "regard the establishment of a naval base, or of a fortified port, in the Persian Gulf by any other power as a very grave menace to British interests," and that it would be resisted "with all the means at our disposal."[56] With Carter's proclamation, the United States was officially putting the world on notice that it was, indeed, assuming the traditional British role of protector in the Gulf region, one that London had abdicated with its withdrawal from the area in 1970–1971.[57]

The capability of the United States at the time to match words with deeds was barely existent, however, and it would be several years into the Reagan administration before the relatively anemic Rapid Deployment Joint Task Force developed by the doctrine evolved into the much more effective Central Command located at MacDill Air Force Base in Tampa, Florida. It was the Central Command that was militarily in charge of operations in the Gulf crisis and war. It was also the Central Command that guided the Kuwaiti reflagging operation in 1987, which, as mentioned previously, was the first serious military commitment, as prescribed by the Carter Doctrine seven years earlier, and the precursor to U.S. involvement in the Gulf in the wake of the Iraqi invasion of Kuwait in August 1990.

The Soviet invasion of Afghanistan put the United States on a war footing in a way it had not known since the days of the Vietnam War. The selective service system was activated just in case a draft became necessary. Analysts, authors, and pundits were dreaming up Third World War scenarios, all focusing on the Persian Gulf region as the likely ignition point. The country seemed weaker than ever, still hamstrung by the Vietnam syndrome and even incapable of rescuing American hostages in Iran. It seemed as though news magazines were publishing frightening numbers every week in the form of graphs depicting how the Soviet Union had moved so far ahead of us in terms of nuclear and conventional military might. A second cold war had begun, but the United States appeared ill prepared to fight it.

This set the stage for Ronald Reagan and a dramatic shift in American politics. One could say that the times had finally caught up (or regressed, depending on one's view of progress and the cold war) with the former governor of California and former presidential candidate. His view of the Soviet Union was a throwback to the Manichean outlook that predominated in the 1950s. Communism was an ideology that had to be resisted by the free nations of the world at all costs, and the Soviet Union was the "evil empire" that was bent on expanding communist influence at the expense of the West all over the globe.

In this sense, the guerrilla/civil wars in places like El Salvador, Nicaragua, Angola, and especially Afghanistan were just as important as NATO's confrontation with the Warsaw Pact, and an active U.S. posture in these Third World proxy conflicts underpinned what came to be known as the Reagan Doctrine.

The United States had to build up its military to match (and possibly exceed) Soviet capabilities, but more importantly, a country still suffering from a bit of an inferiority complex after Vietnam and Watergate had to build up its image. President Carter's election was a reaction against the debacles of the early 1970s. He was a Washington outsider who preached human rights and emphasized a foreign policy based on North-South rather than East-West issues. Although the tremendous increase in military spending of the 1980s actually began during the latter portion of Carter's tenure in office, Ronald Reagan and the Republicans were seen as much better suited to fight the revived cold war. The Soviets had to be turned back at every turn, and Afghanistan became not only the potential launching ground for Moscow's primary threat to Western interests but also the main vehicle for the Reagan administration's resistance to communist expansion, that is, an intensified containment policy.

Turnabout is fair play in politics and diplomacy, and the United States would do what it could to deepen the Afghani quagmire for the Soviets, much as the Soviets did to Americans in Vietnam. But there was one major difference: The dilapidated Soviet economy could not withstand the global pressure that the Reagan administration applied, which only exacerbated the constant drain of the Afghani conflict. As a result, the Soviet Union would first retreat from Afghanistan, and then it would implode. In retrospect, the Soviet invasion in 1979 turned out to be the beginning of the end of the superpower cold war, although at the time there were few who would have predicted this to be the case. Doubt and fear cast a long shadow over the United States in December 1979, preparing the way for an old cold warrior and the Grand Old Party to reenter the mainstream of American politics and foreign policymaking.

Ironically, it was the end of the cold war and disintegration of the Soviet Union, largely brought on, or at least greatly accelerated, by the quagmire in Afghanistan, that allowed the United States to assemble the United Nations–mandated Gulf war coalition in 1990–1991. Gorbachev, in the last days of the existence of the Soviet Union and in the throes of economic and political upheaval, could ill afford to alienate a West that he hoped to tap for investment, aid, and debt relief. Therefore, the Soviets did not veto the anti-Iraqi resolutions in the Security Council and thus enabled the coalition to form. This stands in contrast to the U.S.-led Multinational (not UN) Force that was formed to intervene in Lebanon in 1982, because the Soviets blocked any attempt by the United Nations to sponsor military action that might further reduce their influence in the region and weaken the position of its client-state Syria. Although the Soviet Union did not actively support the UN coalition during the Gulf crisis and war, it did not play the traditional spoiler role characteristic of the cold war, and by default, its relative passivity was a boon to the Bush administration's diplomatic efforts to isolate Iraq in the international community. What the United States determined to be a serious threat to its vital interests in the Gulf region in 1979, as reflected in the Carter Doctrine, actually contributed to the dominant position of the United States in the Persian Gulf area as a result of the Gulf war.

Although a *Pax Americana*, or something close to it, has been established in the Middle East as a result of the primary events of 1979 and their repercussions over the following ten to fifteen years, new threats have emerged in different forms to combat what is seen by some as the political, economic, and sociocultural imperialism of the United States, which has challenged not only political and economic independence on a national scale in the region but also cultural norms and heritage. A prime example of this was a direct result of the Soviet invasion of Afghanistan and the subsequent American response; many would say that this has developed into Washington's own "Frankenstein."

The United States was unprepared and unwilling to directly challenge Moscow's intervention in Afghanistan. This may have been part of the reason for the Carter administration's relative passivity amid signs of a possible Soviet invasion; that is, the United States did not want any empty-threat bluff called by the Kremlin. In order to make it as difficult as possible for the Soviets in Afghanistan, the United States began to support through military and economic aid the *mujahideen*, who had already been fighting the Soviet puppet regimes in Kabul since 1978. The intelligence services of the United States and Saudi Arabia reportedly poured in some $6 billion worth of weapons to the Afghan resistance.[58] Our primary ally in the Indian subcontinent, Pakistan, then under the reign of General Zia al-Haq, became the conduit for U.S. assistance to the *mujahideen*.[59]

Ironically, Iran and the United States shared similar goals in Afghanistan, and as stated previously, Washington hoped for a time that this might create a more propitious environment for the release of the hostages. But Muslim countries the world over rallied to the cause of the *mujahideen*, and Muslim "volunteers" from a plethora of nations began arriving in Afghanistan to lend a hand to the resistance, something the Carter and Reagan administrations encouraged, if not facilitated. Hand-held Stinger anti-aircraft missiles were among the bevy of sophisticated U.S. weaponry that found its way into *mujahideen* hands, anything that would give the rebels a fighting chance, and more importantly from the viewpoint of Washington, ensconce the Soviets deeper into their labyrinth, making it more expensive for the Kremlin to fight the war, much less win it.[60] A CIA-developed "underground railroad" of military aid, primarily through a series of bases established on the Pakistani side of the border with Afghanistan, became a well-honed system of relief and hope for the bedraggled *mujahideen* fighters. The Soviet Union realized within a few years that it would be nearly impossible to achieve total victory against the rebels in a mountainous terrain that provided perfect cover for guerrilla warfare. The Soviet Army might have controlled the major cities, though it was questionable at various times, but it could never subdue the countryside.

As is well known, with the rise to power of Mikhail Gorbachev in 1985, symbolizing a new generation of Soviet leaders who recognized the futility of the conflict and the tremendous economic and increasingly social drain it had on the country, Moscow began to downgrade its involvement in Afghanistan toward total withdrawal by early 1989. Despite oftentimes bitter differences between various *mujahideen* tribal groups, the resistance was successful, due to their tenacity, motivation, strategic knowledge and use of the topography, and substantial aid from the United States as well as other Muslim countries.[61]

With the Soviet withdrawal from Afghanistan and U.S.-U.S.S.R. cooperation in developing resolutions in the United Nations to bring to a close the Iran-Iraq war, the cold war was effectively over, officially consummated with the fall of the Berlin Wall in 1989. The Soviet Union continued to crumble, until out of the ashes of the Soviet empire a new Russia emerged at the end of 1991. Born from the rump of the Soviet Union were a host of new nations in the Baltics, Eastern Europe, and, most importantly for the future of the Middle East, in south-central Asia bordering the traditional regional confines of Turkey and Iran. Muslim countries such as Kazakhstan, Uzbekistan, Tajikistan, Turkmenistan, Kyrgyzstan, and Azerbaijan became new players in Islamic and Middle East politics. Given their strategic position along the old silk route to China and the fact that after the Persian Gulf this region may contain the largest oil reserves in the world, the area inevitably became entangled in a web of international politics, pipelines, and multinational oil companies.

The problem was that not only did the Soviet Union continue to crumble but so did Afghanistan, thoroughly devastated and divided by the war, not unlike Lebanon following the Israeli invasion; more than a million Afghanis perished during the ten-year Soviet occupation, or almost 10 percent of the population. What little infrastructure that existed prior to December 1979 was in tatters. The only real power left after the puppet regime folded upon the Soviet exit was a variety of religious tribal blocs who essentially "duked it out" with one another for a number of years, each group backed by a different coalition of external patrons. Ultimately, the power arising out of this frenetic mix was a group calling itself the Taliban (students), a puritanical Sunni Muslim regime that was determined to restore order to Afghanistan, even if it meant stripping away the heretofore existing freedom and opportunities of Afghani women and the more secularized classes that had emerged during the years of Marxist-Leninist leadership. The breakdown of society had been so thorough that people, at least at first, tended to accept the Taliban simply because they reduced the chaos. Having cast off one decadent secular ideology and superpower already, the accumulated legitimacy of being involved in doing so molded the Taliban into an outpost of Islamic extremism and a lightning rod of Muslim discontent with the West, particularly with the one remaining superpower.[62] The Taliban are the children of the Soviet invasion of Afghanistan, as is "talibanization" the "destabilizing export of Afghan-style radical Islam."[63]

Osama bin Laden, a member of one of the wealthiest families in Saudi Arabia, was one of those volunteers in the 1980s who went to Afghanistan to fight for Islam—and he was also one of those volunteers who were supported by the CIA operations. Now one of the ten most wanted fugitives in the United States, he has allegedly built up a transnational terrorist network (called al-Qaida) and has been accused of numerous terrorist acts against American and other Western targets, most notoriously the bombing of the American embassy compounds in Kenya and Tanzania in 1998 and possibly the al-Khobar bombing on an American base located in Dhahran in the eastern province of Saudi Arabia in 1996, killing nineteen U.S. military personnel.[64] The al-Qaida network has been accused of planning and/or backing operations from China, Chechnya, and India to Jordan, Israel, Saudi Arabia, and even the United States. It is no surprise that after being exiled from Saudi Arabia and hounded out of several other countries, he has now established his safe haven somewhere in Afghanistan.

The incident that transported bin Laden from being a well-known member of the *mujahideen* to an infamous international terrorist was the Western presence in Saudi Arabia during the Gulf crisis and war. Many devout Muslims considered the presence of large numbers of non-Muslims in the country that houses the two most sacred sites in all of Islam (Mecca and Medina) an abomination. To these same Muslims, it only underlined what they viewed as the subservience of the corrupt and hypocritical Saudi regime to the United States and the West. From this fight to rid Saudi Arabia of its infidel presence grew an all-out war against the United States, Israel, and their presumed cohorts in and outside of the Middle East. When the United States departs the Middle East in total and when Israel is destroyed and Jerusalem, the third holiest site in Islam, is restored as the capital of Palestine, then the war will end.

This type of transnational terrorism, intertwined with international weapons smuggling and procurement financed by opium production in Afghanistan, Pakistan, and Lebanon and international money laundering from Russia through Europe and the United States, has changed the nature of global threats in the post–cold war environment, a situation that Washington (and, ironically, Moscow) has only recently come to terms with. The battleground moved to the shores of the United States in 1993, when Islamic radicals trained in Afghanistan carried out the World Trade Center bombings in New York, killing six and injuring more than 1,000, alerting Americans that they were no longer safe from the terror of extremist groups.

The instability in Afghanistan that gave rise to the Taliban has also spilled across the porous borders of the Afghani state toward its neighbors. As Ahmed Rashid comments:

> Into the political vacuum left by 20 years of war and the collapse of stable government has marched a new generation of violent fundamentalists, nurtured and inspired by the Taliban's unique Islamist model. Thousands of foreign radicals now fighting alongside the Taliban in Afghanistan are determined to someday overthrow their own regimes and carry out Taliban-style Islamist revolutions in their homelands. For example, the Chechnya-based militants who took over parts of Dagestan in July [in 1999 in Russia] included in their ranks Arabs, Afghans, and Pakistanis, most of whom had fought in Afghanistan. So had the 800 Uzbek and Tajik gunmen who took over parts of southern Kyrgyzstan in August. The state breakdown in Afghanistan offers militants from Pakistan, Iran, the Central Asian Republics, and China's predominantly Muslim Xinjiang province a tempting package deal: sanctuary and financial support through smuggling.[65]

Beginning with the regime of General Zia al-Haq in the late 1970s and throughout the duration of the Soviet occupation, Pakistan had been the main conduit of supplies earmarked for the *mujahideen*. It also became the primary training ground and sanctuary for Afghanis and Muslims from the Arab world and beyond to fight the Soviets—all supported by the United States and Pakistan and run by their respective intelligence services, the CIA and the Inter-Services Intelligence agency (ISI). Between 1982 and 1992 an estimated 35,000 Muslim radicals from forty Islamic countries joined the Afghani fight, first against the Soviets, then against the rump regime left behind, which finally fell to the *mujahideen* in 1992.[66] From Pakistan alone, between 1994 and 1999, an estimated 80,000–100,000 new followers trained and fought in Afghanistan, primarily to help the Taliban rise to power in 1996 and ward off the opposition (mainly the non-Pushtun Northern Alliance supported by Iran, Russia, India, and many of the former Soviet central Asian republics). Because of this Islamist cross-pollination, the Pakistani regimes of Prime Minister Nawaz Sharif and his successor, General Pervez Musharrif (who overthrew Sharif in October 1999), have been heavily influenced by Islamist parties, particularly in the ISI and in the military.[67] The fact that there were over three million Afghani refugees ensconced in Pakistan by 1988 not only created an economic burden (despite UN relief) for Islamabad but also made it a proving ground for Islamic militancy.[68]

In fact, Musharrif's regime is caught in a dilemma. Although it has been pressured by the international community, primarily the United States, to curtail its support of the Taliban, assist in Washington's efforts to corral Osama bin Laden, and crack down on extremist Islamist groups inside Pakistan, it utilizes, and indeed in many ways depends upon, these very same parties, such as the JUI, Lashkar-e-Toiba, and Harakat al-Mujahideen, to confront India regarding control of Kashmir and other contentious issues between the two countries.[69] Pakistani officials even consider a Taliban-controlled Afghanistan as providing some strategic depth against India in case of war.[70] If the regime does what Washington wants, it risks the unleashing of widespread Islamist opposition in the country; in addition, it loses its shock troops in the struggle over Kashmir. If it continues to support the Taliban and allows domestic Islamist groups to operate as freely as they have, it faces the possibility of having created its own "Frankenstein" coming back to haunt it, possibly taking over the country in essence if not in name. The regime also faces the strong possibility of having international sanctions imposed upon it as a state that sponsors terrorism, while its international credibility continues to erode amid the desperate need for external economic investment, debt relief, and international monetary support.[71]

The Islamist influence inside Pakistan and the support these groups receive from the Taliban and other external sources such as bin Laden's al-Qaida have inestimably raised the level of tension with its neighbor to the east, India. The heightened confrontation has particularly focused on Kashmir, a Muslim-dominated provincial vestige of the imperfect de-colonization of the Indian subcontinent split between the two countries along a very tense international divide called the "Line of Control." Since both India and Pakistan exploded nuclear devices in 1998, thus joining the nuclear club of nations, a conflict between the two, such as that which occurred in 1999 in the so-called Kargil incident in Kashmir, could very easily escalate into a nuclear exchange.

India's passive response to the Soviet invasion in 1979, indeed, its refusal to condemn it, bordered on countenance from the point of view of the Pakistanis and *mujahideen.* This is something they have not forgotten, and it has only added to the vehemence of the opposition of both toward New Delhi. From India's perspective, the enhancement of Pakistan's military capabilities acquired from its closer relationship with both the United States and China (itself feeling threatened by the Soviet invasion and India's implicit support of it) seemed all the more foreboding. As a result, New Delhi sanctioned a military buildup of its own, a cyclical progression that automatically induced the other to respond in kind to the point we have now reached—a nuclear standoff. Unfortunately, the two countries are barely speaking with each other as of this writing, despite the efforts of the Clinton administration to orchestrate a rapprochement. And since there are few, if any, safeguards mutually agreed upon by the two regimes that minimize the chances of a nuclear conflagration, the world has correctly taken notice of the severity of the problem, one that can trace at least part of its origins to the fallout of the 1979 Soviet invasion of Afghanistan.

Furthermore, China's involvement in the Afghani situation, due to its tense relationship with both India and the Soviet Union, helped pry the door open for the entrance of Beijing into the Middle East and South Asia as a major supplier of high-technology weapons, especially in the area of long-range missiles. This greatly complicated the Bush and Clinton administrations' attempts to pass legislation that would normalize trade relations with China, and it has been a significant thorn in the side of U.S.-Chinese relations in general. China's entrance as an arms supplier (along with North Korea) has also heightened the sense of vulnerability of a number of countries in the region, namely, Israel, the Gulf Arab states, and India, to states such as Iran, Syria, and Pakistan, who have acquired various weapons systems from Beijing. China, which has refused to sign onto the international Missile Technology Control Regime, was cited in a CIA report submitted to Congress in August 2000 as actually having expanded its role in providing missile development assistance to Pakistan, Iran, and Libya despite considerable pressure from Washington on Beijing to reduce its missile technology sales.[72] In essence, then, the Soviet invasion of Afghanistan was a significant factor in enhancing China's role in the Middle East.[73]

As briefly mentioned earlier, the drug trade, especially that in opium, from which heroin is processed, has played a vital role in the burgeoning instability emanating from south-central Asia. In fact, much as the diamond trade in Africa has fueled a plethora of civil and interstate conflicts in that war-torn continent, so has opium become the financial palliative of regimes and warlords alike in Afghanistan, Pakistan, the former Soviet Asian republics, and even China. Afghanistan produces three times more opium than the rest of the world combined, 4,600 tons in 1999 according to the UN Drug Control Program.[74] The Taliban coffers are enriched with a 20 percent tax on opium dealers and transporters, and not surprisingly, drug dealers run the country's only banking system.[75] As is the case in Colombia in South America, this level of corruption and "criminalized" economy deleteriously affects economic stability and regime control in the region as a whole. The smuggling trade in opium has thus ballooned in recent years, totaling an estimated $5 billion in the region according to a 1997 World Bank study.[76] Opium production, trade, and smuggling now account for more than 50 percent of the GDP of Afghanistan and many of its neighbors. Concurrent with this has been the growth of drug-related mafias throughout the region, all of whom are major funding sources for the Taliban.[77] This type of dependence on opium production and smuggling has stifled legitimate economic growth in Afghanistan, making it that much harder for it to establish a working economic infrastructure. Indeed, today Afghanistan has only six working factories, whereas prior to the Soviet invasion in 1979 it had 220.[78] Thus, in addition to the exponential increase in the number of heroin addicts across south Asia and into China, economic stagnation and corruption are driving these countries into socioeconomic self-immolation. A vicious cycle is then created as one-party authoritarian regimes, especially in the former Soviet Central Asian republics, raise the level of repression in order to combat these multifarious threats, which, in turn, only increases the appeal of Islamic opposition movements and alternative systems of governance.

The Second Oil Shock

Another significant direct result of the events of 1979 was "the second oil shock." Certainly the Egyptian-Israeli peace treaty was considered by oil analysts and economists to be an element of stability, which is what is ultimately required in the region for the safe transport of and easy access to oil in the Middle East, particularly in the Persian Gulf area, at reasonable prices. But the other primary events of that year and their immediate repercussions had a tremendously unsettling effect on the oil market.

The first oil shock occurred as a result of the 1973 Arab-Israeli war. By the outbreak of the war, the producer nations had finally wrested away control of price and production decisions, and the bulk of the profits, from the Western-owned multinational oil companies. Therefore, the oil weapon, unlike during the 1956 Suez war or the 1967 Arab-Israeli war, could be used by Middle East producers much more effectively. Demand had caught up with supply, creating a tighter oil market, and the multinational oil companies no longer had the ability to shift production to non-Middle Eastern sources as efficiently as they had done during previous oil crises. Before initiating the October war, Anwar Sadat had secured a pledge from Saudi Arabia that it would unleash the oil weapon if Egypt faced dire straits. Toward the end of the war, Israel had successfully gone on the offensive, threatening to obliterate Egypt's gains at the beginning of the conflagration. Saudi Arabia, fulfilling its pledge, abandoned its traditional moderation on OPEC oil policy and joined the hawks within the oil cartel, announcing an embargo against the United States, which, Riyadh hoped, would compel Washington to pressure the Israelis to cease and desist from its advance against Egypt. And indeed it was an important factor in intensifying American pressure on Israel and accelerating Henry Kissinger's whirlwind diplomacy following the war.[79]

An unprepared oil market and global economy panicked, and the price of oil rose almost fourfold, from $3.01 per barrel prior to the outbreak of the war to $11.65 by January 1974. OPEC became a four-letter word in the West, and the oil-rich states of the Middle East became the recipients of perhaps the largest transfer of wealth in a short span of time in history. Saudi Arabia and the Persian Gulf sheikhdoms were no longer Bedouin-dominated backwater states in the Middle East— they moved to front and center in the political spectrum of events across the region.

In the interim period between the first and second oil shocks, the "OPEC countries exercised considerable restraint in their price policy, even at the cost of their own interests, in order to afford the consuming countries the time necessary for the required adjustments."[80] The price of oil during these years stayed relatively constant; in fact, it actually declined in real terms. The consuming states, however, did not take advantage of this lull to develop cogent and viable energy policies. They became quite complacent, and it would take another oil shock to shake the consuming nations of the world, most notably the United States, out of their energy policy doldrums and compel them to deal seriously with the issue.[81]

The price of oil in the second shock actually began to creep upward during the Iranian oil workers strike, which had become a feature of the Iranian Revolution by late 1978. By January and February 1979, daily production had decreased by 3.6 million barrels from September 1978 levels. Although this decrease was less than the 4.2 million barrel dip of the 1973 embargo, the spot market in Rotterdam reacted more acutely, and prices rose by more than 40 percent between January and March 1979.[82] By June, the price per barrel of oil on the spot market rose to $35—though Saudi Arabia's official price was set at $23.50, and by November, the benchmark crude, Saudi Arabian Light, was trading at $41. As Rustow reports:

> Thus in the spring and summer of 1979, the world oil market bustled with unwonted activity. Anxious buyers and hopeful speculators, expect-

ing that the shortage would send prices soaring, bought whatever oil they could get their hands on and paid whatever price was asked. The effect was that of a self-fulfilling prophecy. The frantic buying aggravated the shortage, speculation drove up prices and attracted additional speculators, and rising prices caused yet more panic.[83]

The instability and ensuing drop in oil production due to the Iranian Revolution conspired with the Soviet invasion of Afghanistan by the end of the year (with the subsequent bellicosity emerging from the White House) and the beginning of the Iran-Iraq war in September 1980 to push prices up even further. By January 1980, the price for Saudi crude hit $26 per barrel; by September it was $30. In December OPEC set the maximum price for any OPEC crude at $41 per barrel, and by October 1981, the Saudis raised their official price to $34. The revenues OPEC countries received as a result of the price increase were more than double the 1978 total, and commensurate with this financial bonanza were new ambitious, grandiose development plans that would change the face of many of these states. Together the two oil shocks had wondrous effects on many of the OPEC nations, especially those with large oil reserves and relatively small population bases, particularly the Arab Gulf states. Modern infrastructures were built, and literacy, education, and health care advanced at lightning speed. Countries such as Saudi Arabia, Kuwait, and the United Arab Emirates now had the wherewithal to be taken seriously in Middle East diplomacy, utilizing the purse to buy their entry through financial aid, grants, and charity—and the threat of employing the oil weapon again.

With the wealth now accumulating, many of the oil producers, again especially the Arab Gulf sheikhdoms, constructed intricate welfare states, where, in effect, most basic services, such as heath care, education, and utilities were essentially free. This was noble in one respect, but politically expedient in terms of securing the monarchical rule of respective royal families, in another. In any case, it also endangered the future stability of these states by creating standards of living and expectations that needed to be met in perpetuity. If the price of oil took a sharp turn downward for some reason or if population growth tended to outstrip the capacity of the welfare system, then political and economic unrest could result.

In essence, the worst of both worlds occurred. Oil prices declined precipitously, and population growth rates in many of the oil-producing states remained some of the highest in the world. Political and economic problems have beset these states over the past ten to fifteen years, and they will no doubt have to imaginatively deal with them in the future in order to maintain regime status and socioeconomic stability.

The basic cause of the oil price decline was the adoption of long overdue energy policies by most of the industrialized nations: energy conservation, utilization of alternative sources of energy, and exploration for and production of non-OPEC oil. In addition, the information technology revolution has significantly reduced the chances of panic buying, which played such a vital role in the oil price rise in both oil shocks, and a number of countries have established petroleum reserves in order to weather short-term oil crises. All of these advances, combined with the greediness of several OPEC members in the early 1980s who exceeded their quotas in order to cash in while prices remained high, contributed to a growing supply and eventual oil glut. The decision by Saudi Arabia in 1986 to produce at nearly full capacity in order to drive out non-OPEC oil producers (such as North Sea producers and Mexico) and regain its market share only exacerbated the glut, depressing oil prices for well over the next decade to their lowest real levels in almost thirty years.

Only recently has the price of oil risen to more realistic levels that make economic sense for producers and are tolerable for consumers. It appears that both the producers and consumers have learned the lessons of the second oil shock; that is, the industrialized nations should not become complacent, as they were before 1979, and the oil producers should not push up oil prices to levels that damage the global economy—thus lowering overall demand for oil—and that provide incentives for consuming nations to develop non-OPEC oil, alternative energy sources, and active conservation policies. But this is still a work—a history—in progress.

4

Conclusion

On January 1, 1979, it was reported that the Israeli army halted construction by the right-wing Jewish settler bloc known as Gush Emunim of a Jewish settlement just north of Jerusalem. The year had gotten off to an auspicious start. And some things have not changed over the twenty-two years that have elapsed in the interim. Right-wing Jewish settlers, supported by the conservative wing of the Israeli political establishment, are still trying to legally, and sometimes illegally, house as many of their compatriots in the occupied territories as possible in order to establish facts on the ground and disrupt any process that might lead to substantial territorial concessions by Israel. On March 18, 1979, only about a week before the Egyptian-Israeli peace was signed in Washington, the National Religious Party in Israel threatened to resign from the government unless it received assurances that Israel would retain control over the West Bank and Gaza Strip. Just prior to Israeli Prime Minister Ehud Barak's trip to Camp David in July 2000, ostensibly to sign a final status agreement with the Palestinian National Authority, the Israeli orthodox religious party, Shas, resigned from the government in protest of what it anticipated as too many concessions on the part of the Barak government regarding Israeli-controlled territory to be incorporated in a presumed Palestinian state.

Yet some things do indeed change. On April 5, 1979, a spokesman for the right-wing Likud cabinet in Israel stated that the PLO was a "syndicate of murderers" and would "never be any partner to negotiations with Israel." Although today there may be a number of Israelis who still feel this strongly about the subject, most, even the Likud and orthodox religious faithful, despite the apparent breakdown of the Oslo process in the fall of 2000, have accepted the PLO as a negotiating partner.

Change in the Middle East has thoroughly occurred as a result of the events of 1979. The Egyptian-Israeli peace treaty transformed what had been an environment for an all-out Arab-Israeli conflict into one that necessitated a diplomatic resolution, whatever the merits of the treaty itself and its specific contents. Those Arab states and groups that held fast to the call for the destruction of Israel could no longer realistically hope to do so. Other avenues for achieving more limited objectives had to be adopted, and as time passed negotiated solutions became more and more viable. To those Arab states that were either distant from the Arab-Israeli conflict or reluctant to enter the fray due to the prospects of what could be lost in another regionwide conflagration, the treaty was a diplomatic catharsis; that is, they could keep up the façade of the good fight against Israel, knowing full well it could not develop into a reality as long as the treaty remained intact. The mold had been cast, the barrier overcome, and eventually it would be much easier for other Arab states and the PLO to establish formal and informal relations with Israel since the traditional beacon of the Arab world in the twentieth century had already done so.

At least from the standpoint of the United States, the importance of the treaty and the subsequent close relationship between Cairo and Washington was put on full display during the fallout from the Palestinian al-Aqsa *intifada* launched in September 2000.[1] While several Arab leaders called for a declaration of war against Israel in the wake of the Israeli-Palestinian "mini-war," and while many throughout the Arab world called for the total rupture of any relations that had been established with Israel, Egyptian President Hosni Mubarak took the lead in the region to calm the volatile atmosphere. He hosted a hastily gathered meeting at Sharm al-Shaykh in October that included President Clinton, Jordan's King Abdullah, U.N. Secretary-General Kofi Annan, a European Union representative, Barak, and Arafat. The meeting produced only a shaky and conditional cease-fire arrangement, which did not particularly hold very well, but the gathering did succeed for a time in taking some of the steam out of the growing regional tension.

In addition, Mubarak hosted soon thereafter an emergency Arab League summit meeting where, although the blame for the situation was heaped upon Israel amid inflammatory statements and speeches, he was able, with the support of the Arab Gulf states and other moderate Arab countries, to divert calls for a military response (mostly led by Iraq and Libya) and other suggested modes of action, such as reinstituting the Arab economic boycott of Israel (led by Syria) and breaking off diplomatic relations with Tel Aviv. At the meeting's conclusion, a summit communiqué was issued that held negotiated settlement as the best option for the Palestinians and the Arabs in general. Even though the peace process was at a virtual standstill, Egypt significantly helped to ensure that it could be resumed in the future, even if under some other guise than Oslo.[2]

By the end of 2000, some were purporting that another paradigm, at least in the Arab-Israeli arena, could be forming in the wake of the apparent failure of the Madrid and Oslo processes. If Egypt severs its diplomatic relations with Israel, this could certainly be the case, and the Middle East as a whole could enter an entirely new and more dangerous stage of history.[3] If this were to occur and the Middle East were to return to more of a war footing in the Arab-Israeli dimension, then one of the central themes of this book would need to be revised, or at least interpreted in another fashion: The 1979 peace treaty inaugurated a paradigmatic shift, the consequences of which—the failure of the peace process—led to another paradigmatic shift away from the path of a negotiated solution. The analyses of the other two important events of 1979—the Iranian revolution and the Soviet invasion of Afghanistan—would still hold, and, indeed, those events could be seen as having contributed to the failure of the one paradigm and influencing the shape of the new one. Apart from steering the Middle East in a new direction, the Egyptian-Israeli peace treaty might be seen a hundred years from now as eliciting little but a brief respite in a continuing Arab-Israeli conflict.

On the other hand, the Egyptian-Israeli relationship has weathered a number of storms, particularly the 1982 Israeli invasion of Lebanon, when Cairo also recalled its ambassador—and it will probably hold fast through the torrent that began with the al-Aqsa *intifada.* Egypt is as economically dependent on the United States and the monetary institutions and investors in the West as it has ever been, and despite lingering problems, it has made some significant economic structural improvements that have brought it to the cusp of being a model of economic development in the region. Outside of the unlikely occurrence of an Iran-type revolution, Egypt is in no position to abandon the path that it set for itself in 1979. This would suggest, then, that the paradigmatic shift in the Arab-Israeli arena brought about by the Egyptian-Israeli peace treaty still holds true, that is, that a diplomatic resolution of the Arab-Israeli conflict is the only viable alternative for the Arab states and for the Palestinians. However, a new subset within the paradigm, that is, another peace process based on different actors, rationales, and timetables, may result, as has often happened in the past when circumstances have changed, from the original intent of the peace treaty itself to the Reagan, Fahd, Fez, Schulz, and Shamir peace plans of the 1980s and the Madrid and Oslo peace processes of the 1990s.

Along with what many perceive to have been the good also came what many perceive to have been the bad. The worst fears of those in the Arab world who vehemently criticized Sadat for making peace with the Jewish state came to fruition as a three-pronged monster: Israeli acceleration of settlement building in the remaining occupied territories, neglect of the Palestinian issue, and most disastrously, the Israeli invasion of Lebanon in 1982. In addition, the disruption caused by the removal of Egypt from the Arab fold divided the Arab states in a way that had not been experienced since the height of the Arab cold war. The resulting vacuum of power in the inter-Arab arena opened the door for other aspirants to the Egyptian Arab nationalist mantle. Saddam Hussein in Iraq had long waited for this opportunity, and with the new threat emanating from Teheran, he leapt after it in a bold, yet ultimately catastrophic fashion, initiating one war, the results of which laid the foundation for another.

The Iranian revolution disrupted the "other" arena in the Middle East—the Persian Gulf—but it had reverberations throughout the region. During the early years of the revolution, while still in its dynamic period, Iran raised the banner of Islamic opposition and resistance to Western imperialism, Israel, and impious Muslims who had sold out to the West. It set the standard for Islamic change in a region that was experiencing a vast amount of change overall, from tremendous wealth gathering in some states to growing poverty and corruption in others, from a tradition of pan-Arab unity to increasing balkanization, and from exhilaration and hope to frustration and despair.[4] In the gaps of these mountains of change were wellsprings of discontented recruits—in Lebanon, Iraq, Bahrain, Saudi Arabia, Egypt, and so on. The revolution was an Islamic one, and not just an Iranian one, until the late 1980s, when the war with Iraq and the death of Khomeini in 1989 forced the mullahs into a more pragmatic foreign policy stance. During its "volcanic" stage, it lit a fire under the Middle East just when it seemed the Egyptian-Israeli peace treaty was putting out the biggest bonfire of them all. The instability inserted into the region and its aftershocks are still being felt today, as one can draw a direct line from the fall of the Shah through the Iran-Iraq war to the Gulf war and beyond. The nature of the revolution has gradually changed over the years, and Iran today, especially after the landslide election of the pro-reformist moderate President Muhammad Khatami in 1997, is struggling somewhat with its identity. Is it still the Iran of Khomeini, or is it the Khatami Iran of a new generation tired of war, instability, and international isolation? Or will some sort of hybrid, what Lou Cantori termed, a "shurocracy," develop that will point the way toward a legitimate Islamic alternative to the democratic capitalist wave that has enveloped the globe in the aftermath of the cold war?[5]

The Soviet invasion of Afghanistan left a country in ruins. In the wake of the breakup of the Soviet Union and the ensuing severe political and economic problems experienced by the new Russian Federation, one might ask which nation was actually "ruined" by the conflict. It is clear, however, that the physical devastation of Afghanistan was enormous. As in the environments created by the Egyptian-Israeli peace treaty and the fall of the Shah, vacuums of power create opportunities that are immediately seized upon. The Islamist opposition to the Soviet occupation mutated into the Taliban in the chaotic aftermath of the Red Army withdrawal. The Taliban was itself a mutation of a puritanical form of Sunni Islamism whose thunder has since been felt throughout South and Central Asia. Just as the Soviet exit generated instability in Afghanistan, so has the end of the Soviet empire acted as a conduit for the spread of Taliban influence in Muslim-dominated Central Asia. The vehicles for assisting the *mujahideen* have also evolved into varying degrees of torment for those who manufactured them. In the person of Osama bin Laden, the South and Central Asian, Persian Gulf, and Arab-Israeli arenas have been culled together in terms of extremist Islamist opposition; Hizbullah in Lebanon and the Palestinian Islamist organizations, Hamas and Islamic Jihad, have reportedly established deeper links with bin Laden's group in the past year or so as al-Qaida has extended its interests and influence into the Arab-Israeli arena seeking to disrupt the peace process.[6] The terrorist bombing during the al-Aqsa *intifada* of the USS *Cole* on a refueling operation in Yemen on October 12, 2000, killing seventeen U.S. sailors, in which Osama bin Laden is a prime suspect, underscored the regional nature of the threat. It is suspected that the actual operation was carried out by some "Afghan Arabs" of Yemeni origin, i.e., Yemenis who had fought as volunteers with the *mujahideen* in Afghanistan who have since aligned themselves with Islamic extremist organizations such as bin Laden's.[7] In a sense, the increase in tension and the heightened potential destructiveness of any devolution into confrontation between India and Pakistan, the global operations of the transnational Islamist "terrorist" groups linked with the regime in Kabul and/or Osama bin Laden, and the preparations by those targeted by Islamic extremists are all subsets of the Soviet invasion.

As were the changing political, economic, and cultural landscapes of the two superpowers. The one reeled from the quagmire it had gotten itself into, eventually imploding from the gap between being a military superpower and an economic pygmy—the latter in no way, shape, or form in any position to support the former, especially when its sworn enemy raised the bar of the cold war conflict in the Third World. The other, itself reeling from its own recent military morass, found redemption in the opportunity to best its superpower rival in a match it knew it would win, for it could play the cold war game at a much higher level of engagement. A second cold war ushered in a new political, military, and economic philosophy for over a decade, the influence of which still plays a significant role in the determination of elections from the presidency down to the municipal level. The result was the end of the cold war and an end to the Soviet Union. We are still trying to figure out what exactly has emerged in the post–cold war environment, but one thing is for sure: The Manichean simplicity of the superpower standoff has been replaced by something that is much more complex, multidimensional, interdependent, and possibly fraught with just as much danger.

On a more general level, one clearly observable repercussion of the events of 1979 is that the center of gravity in the Middle East has steadily moved eastward toward the Persian Gulf and the Indian subcontinent. The oil embargo during the 1973 Arab-Israeli war and the ensuing power of OPEC popularly linked the Persian Gulf arena with events in the eastern Mediterranean. However, with the abdication of Egypt in 1979 occurring, in historical terms, practically simultaneously with the Iranian revolution and the Soviet invasion of Afghanistan, the focus for policymakers, the interested public, and many academicians shifted eastward toward areas that heretofore had received scant treatment. Even though events in the Arab-Israeli arena would continue to attract a good deal of attention, and at times even more, as in the case of the Israeli invasion of Lebanon, the hostage crisis in Beirut, the 1987 and 2000 Palestinian *intifadas*, and various peace plans floated about from time to time, it was existentially not quite the same as it had been prior to 1979. Two-thirds of the known oil reserves are in the Persian Gulf region, where Washington's trusted ally had just been overthrown and where a destructive war was about to begin. The second cold war had been initiated in the mountains of Afghanistan, and the preferred location among World War III prognosticators for the beginning of the potential nuclear holocaust was the Persian Gulf. Iraq ambitiously seized the mantle of Arab leadership from Egypt. The new regime in Teheran said it spoke for and represented Muslims everywhere in its sometimes successful attempts to transform its revolution into a dynamic pan-Islamic movement. The Arab Gulf states, with the formation of the GCC, had taken it upon themselves to look after the matters that affected them most, basically admitting they had little in common with the rest of the Arab world to the west.

Eventually the activation of the regime in Baghdad in 1979 would lead to its invasion of Kuwait in 1990, inviting the wrath of the world's most powerful country (which needed to prove to itself that it actually was) and bringing together a coalition of countries that in its composition was an imprint of the end of the cold war and Arab-Israeli conflict. The victory of the *mujahideen* and the uncorking of Central Asia and the Indian subcontinent would politically, economically, and religiously link the Middle East even further eastward, up and through the Black Sea and Caspian Sea basins all the way into China. The connective nature of the old "silk route" of medieval Islamic times seems to have been reborn, except that the goods being traded today, though just as valuable, are much more dangerous and destabilizing: arms, drugs, and ideology.

Until there is a working comprehensive agreement, Arab-Israeli issues will always have the potential to periodically revert world attention westward. But as long as Egypt and Israel remain at peace and progress on the Palestinian front is more fact than fiction, events eastward will continue to command more of center stage. This is, by the way, not necessarily a good thing, for global attention tends to be focused on events of an unsettling nature: war, terrorism, political rupture, and diplomatic confrontation. But then again it is that very same attention that, unfortunately, seems to be necessary in order to garner the domestic, regional, and international focus and energy toward peaceful resolution. The Egyptian-Israeli peace treaty is a prime example.

Nevertheless, it is important to point out that although events in the Persian Gulf and Indian subcontinent regions have garnered a great deal of attention since 1979 (an assertion most recently reinforced by President Clinton's trip to both India and Pakistan in the spring of 2000 in an attempt to reduce the level of tension and persuade the regime in Islamabad to combat the extremism emanating from Taliban-controlled Afghanistan), the Arab-Israeli arena, particularly the Palestinian issue, remains very important, as evidenced by the effort exerted by the Clinton administration in arranging the Camp David meeting in August 2000 (although Clinton's critics have argued that the effort was less about the fruits of peace and more about securing a Clintonian legacy). The Clinton administration learned, the hard way, that its strategic objectives in the Persian Gulf, particularly those of containing Saddam Hussein and stabilizing oil prices, are tied to progress on the Palestinian problem and an overall Arab-Israeli agreement. To acquire the necessary support from the Gulf and other Arab states for its policy vis-à-vis Iraq, the United States had to press forward more aggressively on the Arab-Israeli front on issues that are still salient in the Arab world as a whole. This is not to say that the U.S. role in the Arab-Israeli peace process is solely a function of the Persian Gulf arena, but the two are intimately related.

During the cold war, the primary objectives of the United States in the Middle East were threefold: prevent the expansion of Soviet influence, promote stability in the Persian Gulf in order to maintain the safe transport of and easy access to oil at reasonable prices, and protect Israel. The cold war is over and the Soviet Union has evaporated, so that objective is no longer operative. The Egyptian-Israeli peace treaty and the subsequent regional reconfiguration following the Gulf war that led to, inter alia, the 1993 Israeli-PLO Declaration of Principles and the 1994 Jordanian-Israeli peace treaty has immeasurably improved Israel's security, to the extent that the traditional U.S. objective of protecting Israel (and/or providing it with the means to protect itself), while not insignificant, merits less concern. Of the original three objectives, this leaves one: stability in the Persian Gulf. And it remains a very high priority (and not just to the United States), although the problems surrounding the central and south Asian regions have climbed steadily to the top portions of the ladder in recent years. During the cold war era, the Arab-Israeli peace process was determined by many in Washington to have been a means to an end, that is, a way to achieve the three aforementioned primary policy objectives. Today it can still be viewed as a means to an end, but it is probably more a function of the Persian Gulf arena than ever before. If one accepts this premise, the logical conclusion in the context of this discussion reaffirms the notion that the center of gravity in the Middle East has moved eastward.

Why did the pertinent events of 1979 in the Middle East occur at virtually the same moment? Were there underlying forces of some sort that all of a sudden randomly came together, just as the buildup of pressure along fault lines from tectonic shifts eventually results in earthquakes? Although, as delineated in Chapter 2, there were a number of interrelationships, some of them fairly important, among the three primary events of 1979, for the most part the circumstances of their origins were quite divergent and unrelated; therefore, it is difficult, if not impossible, to offer any general theory of relativity on the subject.

Let me offer one possible explanation that may be worth a moment or two of contemplation. What might have induced the environment in which the events of 1979 took place is the convergence of what I call the loss of promise. The promise of liberating Palestine and pushing the Jewish state into the sea was no longer viable for the Arab world. It had become a pipe dream or, at least in the determination of most (particularly Egypt), not worth the effort. The damage sustained in and the potential destructiveness demonstrated by the 1973 Arab-Israeli war convinced many that one of the unifying themes of Arab nationalism could no longer be maintained. Strategic and diplomatic alternatives were thus adopted, both of which took for granted the continued existence of Israel. Egypt was simply in position first, under the right type of leadership, to "cross over" to the other side of a very different divide and choose a negotiated settlement.[8]

In Iran under the Shah, the promise had been one of systemic improvement in the condition of life of all Iranians, supposedly stemming from the tremendous rise in oil revenues induced by the 1973 Arab-Israeli war. Although the GNP continued to rise year after year, the distribution of that wealth became more and more narrow, and the economic and cultural gap between the rich and poor widened—while the Shah's megalomania and myopia grew. The resulting discontent coalesced into revolution, beginning a new promise to the Iranian population, which is today coming under increasing scrutiny. That this occurred in the late 1970s may not be entirely accidental. In many of the Third World postcolonial regimes, whether of socialist, authoritarian, or monarchic orientation, the promise of real socioeconomic and/or political progress had proven hollow, and they had all but exhausted the goodwill gained and/or manufactured in the early years of their rule. The statute of limitations on fulfilling their promises had expired. Judgment day for a number of regimes had come—they needed to make good on their promises, or move, or be pushed, aside. The friction generated by opposition movements of one form or another from Central and Latin America to the Middle East to Southeast Asia produced explosive conditions in many states. In some places, the repressive apparatus of the state, as in Syria, Guatemala, and the Philippines, was sufficient to hold back or eliminate the rising tide of discontent; in others, such as Nicaragua and Iran, the opposition was much more successful. The friction was, in part, a function of the cold war, but for the most part, it was based on indigenous forces that created opportunities for intervention by the superpowers, only exacerbating pre-existing fissures in the process.

The Soviet invasion of Afghanistan may have resulted from the unfulfilled promise of détente with the United States. It was clear that what had been a policy priority for both Moscow and Washington in the late 1960s and early 1970s had substantially unraveled well before December 1979. Indeed, the intimate involvement of the two superpowers on opposing sides in the 1973 Arab-Israeli war, despite summit pledges not to do so, and the near-nuclear confrontation in the waning stages of the conflict, showed the limitations of détente. The cold war had apparently become too institutionalized to be cast aside by a few summit meetings, hugs between leaders, economic deals, and arms limitation (rather than reduction) talks. In the fall of 1979, the Kremlin felt it had little to lose in terms of its relationship with the United States, especially as Washington was improving its ties with Beijing. Détente was an illusion, something that most Americans would agree with by the end of the year. When illusions are revealed, the reactions can be swift and intense, and in both the Soviet Union and in the United States, they were. Promises could not end the cold war—someone had to lose.

This supposition is plausible only in the broadest sense, and it functions as only a partial explanation for the occurrence of these events during the same period of time, that is, within about a decade of each other (it is similar to Elton's situational causes outlined in Chapter 1). As to all three events taking place within the same calendar year, this cannot be determined with any legitimate specificity; chance and individual whim had more to do with it than anything else. Certainly the Iranian revolution and the ensuing deterioration of relations between Washington and Teheran, as mentioned in Chapter 2, had some effect upon the Kremlin in terms of the timing of its decision to invade Afghanistan. Beyond this, each primary event of 1979 had a life of its own. Nevertheless, the actors in each event would meet at various interstices of history down the road and together indelibly leave their marks. Gazing down from the mountain peaks of history, one might perceive the world as either better or worse after the tumult of 1979, but one could not deny that it was most certainly different. The Middle East, indeed, the world, had changed—we just didn't know it yet.

APPENDIX A

The Camp David Accords:
The Framework for Peace
in the Middle East

Muhammad Anwar al-Sadat, President of the Arab Republic of Egypt, and Menachem Begin, Prime Minister of Israel, met with Jimmy Carter, President of the United States of America, at Camp David from September 5 to September 17, 1978, and have agreed on the following framework for peace in the Middle East. They invite other parties to the Arab-Israel conflict to adhere to it.

Preamble

The search for peace in the Middle East must be guided by the following:

- The agreed basis for a peaceful settlement of the conflict between Israel and its neighbors is United Nations Security Council Resolution 242, in all its parts.
- After four wars during 30 years, despite intensive human efforts, the Middle East, which is the cradle of civilization and the birthplace of three great religions, does not enjoy the blessings of peace. The people of the Middle East yearn for peace so that the vast human and natural resources of the region can be turned to the pursuits of peace and so that this area can become a model for coexistence and cooperation among nations.
- The historic initiative of President Sadat in visiting Jerusalem and the reception accorded to him by the parliament, govern-

ment and people of Israel, and the reciprocal visit of Prime Minister Begin to Ismailia, the peace proposals made by both leaders, as well as the warm reception of these missions by the peoples of both countries, have created an unprecedented opportunity for peace which must not be lost if this generation and future generations are to be spared the tragedies of war.

- The provisions of the Charter of the United Nations and the other accepted norms of international law and legitimacy now provide accepted standards for the conduct of relations among all states.

- To achieve a relationship of peace, in the spirit of Article 2 of the United Nations Charter, future negotiations between Israel and any neighbor prepared to negotiate peace and security with it are necessary for the purpose of carrying out all the provisions and principles of Resolutions 242 and 338.

- Peace requires respect for the sovereignty, territorial integrity and political independence of every state in the area and their right to live in peace within secure and recognized boundaries free from threats or acts of force. Progress toward that goal can accelerate movement toward a new era of reconciliation in the Middle East marked by cooperation in promoting economic development, in maintaining stability and in assuring security.

- Security is enhanced by a relationship of peace and by cooperation between nations which enjoy normal relations. In addition, under the terms of peace treaties, the parties can, on the basis of reciprocity, agree to special security arrangements such as demilitarized zones, limited armaments areas, early warning stations, the presence of international forces, liaison, agreed measures for monitoring and other arrangements that they agree are useful.

Framework

Taking these factors into account, the parties are determined to reach a just, comprehensive, and durable settlement of the Middle East conflict through the conclusion of peace treaties based on Security Council resolutions 242 and 338 in all their parts. Their purpose is to achieve peace and good neighborly relations. They recognize that for peace to endure, it must involve all those who have been most deeply affected by the conflict. They therefore agree that this framework, as appropriate, is intended by them to constitute a basis for peace not only between Egypt and Israel, but also between Israel and each of its other neighbors which is prepared to negotiate peace with Israel on this basis. With that objective in mind, they have agreed to proceed as follows:

A. West Bank and Gaza

1. Egypt, Israel, Jordan and the representatives of the Palestinian people should participate in negotiations on the resolution of the Palestinian problem in all its aspects. To achieve that objective, negotiations relating to the West Bank and Gaza should proceed in three stages:

    a. Egypt and Israel agree that, in order to ensure a peaceful and orderly transfer of authority, and taking into account the security concerns of all the parties, there should be transitional arrangements for the West Bank and Gaza for a period not exceeding five years. In order to provide full autonomy to the inhabitants, under these arrangements the Israeli military government and its civilian administration will be withdrawn as soon as a self-governing authority has been freely elected by the inhabitants of these areas to replace the existing military government. To negotiate the details of a transitional arrangement, Jordan will be invited to join the negotiations on the basis of this framework. These new arrangements should give due consideration both to the principle of self-government by the inhabitants of these territories and to the legitimate security concerns of the parties involved.

    b. Egypt, Israel, and Jordan will agree on the modalities for establishing elected self governing authority in the West Bank and Gaza. The delegations of Egypt and Jordan may include Palestinians from the West Bank and Gaza or other Palestinians as mutually agreed. The parties will negotiate an agreement which will define the powers and responsibilities of the self-governing authority to be exercised in the West Bank and Gaza. A withdrawal of Israeli armed forces will take place and there will be a redeployment of the remaining Israeli forces into specified security locations. The agreement will also include arrangements for assuring internal and external security and public order. A strong local police force will be established, which may include Jordanian citizens. In addition, Israeli and Jordanian forces will participate in joint patrols and in the manning of control posts to assure the security of the borders.

c. When the self-governing authority (administrative council) in the West Bank and Gaza is established and inaugurated, the transitional period of five years will begin. As soon as possible, but not later than the third year after the beginning of the transitional period, negotiations will take place to determine the final status of the West Bank and Gaza and its relationship with its neighbors and to conclude a peace treaty between Israel and Jordan by the end of the transitional period. These negotiations will be conducted among Egypt, Israel, Jordan and the elected representatives of the inhabitants of the West Bank and Gaza. Two separate but related committees will be convened, one committee, consisting of representatives of the four parties which will negotiate and agree on the final status of the West Bank and Gaza, and its relationship with its neighbors, and the second committee, consisting of representatives of Israel and representatives of Jordan to be joined by the elected representatives of the inhabitants of the West Bank and Gaza, to negotiate the peace treaty between Israel and Jordan, taking into account the agreement reached in the final status of the West Bank and Gaza. The negotiations shall be based on all the provisions and principles of UN Security Council Resolution 242. The negotiations will resolve, among other matters, the location of the boundaries and the nature of the security arrangements. The solution from the negotiations must also recognize the legitimate right of the Palestinian peoples and their just requirements. In this way, the Palestinians will participate in the determination of their own future through:

i. The negotiations among Egypt, Israel, Jordan and the representatives of the inhabitants of the West Bank and Gaza to agree on the final status of the West Bank and Gaza and other outstanding issues by the end of the transitional period.

ii. Submitting their agreements to a vote by the elected representatives of the inhabitants of the West Bank and Gaza.

iii. Providing for the elected representatives of the inhabitants of the West Bank and Gaza to decide how they shall govern themselves consistent with the provisions of their agreement.

iv. Participating as stated above in the work of the committee negotiating the peace treaty between Israel and Jordan.

2. All necessary measures will be taken and provisions made to assure the security of Israel and its neighbors during the transitional period and beyond. To assist in providing such security, a strong local police force will be constituted by the self-governing authority. It will be composed of inhabitants of the West Bank and Gaza. The police will maintain liaison on internal security matters with the designated Israeli, Jordanian, and Egyptian officers.

3. During the transitional period, representatives of Egypt, Israel, Jordan, and the self-governing authority will constitute a continuing committee to decide by agreement on the modalities of admission of persons displaced from the West Bank and Gaza in 1967, together with necessary measures to prevent disruption and disorder. Other matters of common concern may also be dealt with by this committee.

4. Egypt and Israel will work with each other and with other interested parties to establish agreed procedures for a prompt, just and permanent implementation of the resolution of the refugee problem.

B. Egypt-Israel

1. Egypt-Israel undertake not to resort to the threat or the use of force to settle disputes. Any disputes shall be settled by peaceful

means in accordance with the provisions of Article 33 of the U.N. Charter.

2. In order to achieve peace between them, the parties agree to negotiate in good faith with a goal of concluding within three months from the signing of the Framework a peace treaty between them while inviting the other parties to the conflict to proceed simultaneously to negotiate and conclude similar peace treaties with a view the* achieving a comprehensive peace in the area. The Framework for the Conclusion of a Peace Treaty between Egypt and Israel will govern the peace negotiations between them. The parties will agree on the modalities and the timetable for the implementation of their obligations under the treaty.

C. Associated Principles

1. Egypt and Israel state that the principles and provisions described below should apply to peace treaties between Israel and each of its neighbors—Egypt, Jordan, Syria and Lebanon.

2. Signatories shall establish among themselves relationships normal to states at peace with one another. To this end, they should undertake to abide by all the provisions of the U.N. Charter. Steps to be taken in this respect include:

   a. full recognition

   b. abolishing economic boycotts

   c. guaranteeing that under their jurisdiction the citizens of the other parties shall enjoy the protection of the due process of law.

3. Signatories should explore possibilities for economic development in the context of final peace treaties, with the objective of contributing to the atmosphere of peace, cooperation and friendship which is their common goal.

4. Claims commissions may be established for the mutual settlement of all financial claims.

5. The United States shall be invited to participated in the talks on matters related to the modalities of the implementation of the

---

*Typographical errors in this document appeared in the original one.

agreements and working out the timetable for the carrying out of the obligations of the parties.

6. The United Nations Security Council shall be requested to endorse the peace treaties and ensure that their provisions shall not be violated. The permanent members of the Security Council shall be requested to underwrite the peace treaties and ensure respect or the provisions. They shall be requested to conform their policies an actions with the undertaking contained in this Framework.

For the Government of the
Arab Republic of Egypt:
Muhammed Anwar al-Sadat

For the Government
of Israel:
Menachem Begin

Witnessed by:
Jimmy Carter, President of the United States of America

Framework for the Conclusion of a Peace Treaty between Egypt and Israel

In order to achieve peace between them, Israel and Egypt agree to negotiate in good faith with a goal of concluding within three months of the signing of this framework a peace treaty between them:
It is agreed that:

- The site of the negotiations will be under a United Nations flag at a location or locations to be mutually agreed.
- All of the principles of U.N. Resolution 242 will apply in this resolution of the dispute between Israel and Egypt.
- Unless otherwise mutually agreed, terms of the peace treaty will be implemented between two and three years after the peace treaty is signed.

The following matters are agreed between the parties:

1. the full exercise of Egyptian sovereignty up to the internationally recognized border between Egypt and mandated Palestine;
2. the withdrawal of Israeli armed forces from the Sinai;
3. the use of airfields left by the Israelis near al-Arish, Rafah, Ras en-Naqb, and Sharm el-Sheikh for civilian purposes only, including possible commercial use only by all nations;
4. the right of free passage by ships of Israel through the Gulf of Suez and the Suez Canal on the basis of the Constantinople Convention of 1888 applying to all nations; the Strait of Tiran and Gulf of Aqaba are international waterways to be open to all nations for unimpeded and nonsuspendable freedom of navigation and overflight;
5. the construction of a highway between the Sinai and Jordan near Eilat with guaranteed free and peaceful passage by Egypt and Jordan; and
6. the stationing of military forces listed below.

Stationing of Forces

- No more than one division (mechanized or infantry) of Egyptian armed forces will be stationed within an area lying approximately 50 km. (30 miles) east of the Gulf of Suez and the Suez Canal.
- Only United Nations forces and civil police equipped with light weapons to perform normal police functions will be stationed within an area lying west of the international border and the Gulf of Aqaba, varying in width from 20 km. (12 miles) to 40 km. (24 miles).
- In the area within 3 km. (1.8 miles) east of the international border there will be Israeli limited military forces not to exceed four infantry battalions and United Nations observers.
- Border patrol units not to exceed three battalions will supplement the civil police in maintaining order in the area not included above.
- The exact demarcation of the above areas will be as decided during the peace negotiations.

- Early warning stations may exist to insure compliance with the terms of the agreement. United Nations forces will be stationed:
1. in part of the area in the Sinai lying within about 20 km. of the Mediterranean Sea and adjacent to the international border, and
2. in the Sharm el-Sheikh area to insure freedom of passage through the Strait of Tiran; and these forces will not be removed unless such removal is approved by the Security Council of the United Nations with a unanimous vote of the five permanent members.

- After a peace treaty is signed, and after the interim withdrawal is complete, normal relations will be established between Egypt and Israel, including full recognition, including diplomatic, economic and cultural relations; termination of economic boycotts and barriers to the free movement of goods and people; and mutual protection of citizens by the due process of law.

Interim Withdrawal

Between three months and nine months after the signing of the peace treaty, all Israeli forces will withdraw east of a line extending from a point east of El-Arish to Ras Muhammad, the exact location of this line to be determined by mutual agreement.

For the Government of the
Arab Republic of Egypt:
Muhammed Anwar al-Sadat

For the Government
of Israel:
Menachem Begin

Witnessed by:
Jimmy Carter, President of the United States of America

**Author's Note: In addition to the above text there was an "Annex to the Framework Agreements" consisting of "Exchanges of Letters" between Carter, Sadat, and Begin further delineating and/or clarifying various aspects of the accords.

APPENDIX B

*Peace Treaty Between
Egypt and Israel*

March 26, 1979

The Government of the Arab Republic of Egypt and the Government of the State of Israel;

Preamble

Convinced of the urgent necessity of the establishment of a just, comprehensive and lasting peace in the Middle East in accordance with Security Council Resolutions 242 and 338;

Reaffirming their adherence to the "Framework for Peace in the Middle East Agreed at Camp David." dated September 17, 1978;

Noting that the aforementioned Framework as appropriate is intended to constitute a basis for peace not only between Egypt and Israel but also between Israel and each of its other Arab neighbors which is prepared to negotiate peace with it on this basis;

Desiring to bring to an end the state of war between them and to establish a peace in which every state in the area can live in security;

Convinced that the conclusion of a Treaty of Peace between Egypt and Israel is an important step in the search for comprehensive peace in the area and for the attainment of settlement of the Arab-Israeli conflict in all its aspects;

Inviting the other Arab parties to this dispute to join the peace process with Israel guided by and based on the principles of the aforementioned Framework;

Desiring as well to develop friendly relations and cooperation between themselves in accordance with the United Nations Charter and the principles of international law governing international relations in times of peace;

Agree to the following provisions in the free exercise of their sovereignty, in order to implement the "Framework for the Conclusion of a Peace Treaty Between Egypt and Israel";

Article I

1. The state of war between the Parties will be terminated and peace will be established between them upon the exchange of instruments of ratification of this Treaty.
2. Israel will withdraw all its armed forces and civilians from the Sinai behind the international boundary between Egypt and mandated Palestine, as provided in the annexed protocol (Annex I), and Egypt will resume the exercise of its full sovereignty over the Sinai.
3. Upon completion of the interim withdrawal provided for in Annex I, the parties will establish normal and friendly relations, in accordance with Article III (3).

Article II

The permanent boundary between Egypt and Israel in* the recognized international boundary between Egypt and the former mandated territory of Palestine, as shown on the map at Annex II, without prejudice to the issue of the status of the Gaza Strip. The Parties recognize this boundary as inviolable. Each will respect the territorial integrity of the other, including their territorial waters and airspace.

Article III

1. The Parties will apply between them the provisions of the Charter of the United Nations and the principles of international law governing relations among states in times of peace. In particular:

   a. They recognize and will respect each other's sovereignty, territorial integrity and political independence;

---

*Typographical errors in this document appeared in the original one.

b. They recognize and will respect each other's right to live in peace within their secure and recognized boundaries;

c. They will refrain from the threat or use of force, directly or indirectly, against each other and will settle all disputes between them by peaceful means.

2. Each Party undertakes to ensure that acts or threats of belligerency, hostility, or violence do not originate from and are not committed from within its territory, or by any forces subject to its control or by any other forces stationed on its territory , against the population, citizens or property of the other Party. Each Party also undertakes to refrain from organizing, instigating, inciting, assisting or participating in acts or threats of belligerency, hostility, subversion or violence against the other Party, anywhere, and undertakes to ensure that perpetrators of such acts are brought to justice.

3. The Parties agree that the normal relationship established between them will include full recognition, diplomatic, economic and cultural relations, termination of economic boycotts and discriminatory barriers to the free movement of people and goods, and will guarantee the mutual enjoyment by citizens of the due process of law. The process by which they undertake to achieve such a relationship parallel to the implementation of other provisions of this Treaty is set out in the annexed protocol (Annex III).

Article IV

1. In order to provide maximum security for both Parties on the basis of reciprocity, agreed security arrangements will be established including limited force zones in Egyptian and Israeli territory, and United Nations forces and observers, described in detail as to nature and timing in Annex I, and other security arrangements the Parties may agree upon.

2. The Parties agree to the stationing of United Nations personnel in areas described in Annex I. The Parties agree not to request withdrawal of the United Nations personnel and that these personnel will not be removed unless such removal is approved by

the Security Council of the United Nations, with the affirmative vote of the five Permanent Members, unless the Parties otherwise agree.

3. A Joint Commission will be established to facilitate the implementation of the Treaty, as provided for in Annex I.

4. The security arrangements provided for in paragraphs 1 and 2 of this Article may at the request of either party be reviewed and amended by mutual agreement of the Parties.

Article V

1. Ships of Israel, and cargoes destined for or coming from Israel, shall enjoy the right of free passage through the Suez Canal and its approaches through the Gulf of Suez and the Mediterranean Sea on the basis of the Constantinople Convention of 1888, applying to all nations, Israeli nationals, vessels and cargoes, as well as persons, vessels and cargoes destined for or coming from Israel, shall be accorded non-discriminatory treatment in all matters connected with usage of the canal.

2. The Parties consider the Strait of Tiran and. the Gulf of Aqaba to be international waterways open to all nations for unimpeded and non-suspendable freedom of navigation and overflight.

3. The parties will respect each other's right to navigation and overflight for access to either country through the Strait of Tiran and the Gulf of Aqaba.

Article VI

1. This Treaty does not affect and shall not be interpreted as affecting in any way the rights and obligations of the Parties under the Charter of the United Nations.

2. The Parties undertake to fulfill in good faith their obligations under this Treaty, without regard to action or inaction of any other party and independently of any instrument external to this Treaty.

3. They further undertake to take all the necessary measures for the application in their relations of the provisions of the multilateral conventions to which they are parties, including the sub-

mission of appropriate notification to the Secretary General of the United Nations and other depositaries of such conventions.

4. The Parties undertake not to enter into any obligation in conflict with this Treaty.

5. Subject to Article 103 of the United Nations Charter in the event of a conflict between the obligation of the Parties under the present Treaty and any of their other obligations, the obligations under this Treaty will be binding and implemented.

Article VII

1. Disputes arising out of the application or interpretation of this Treaty shall be resolved by negotiations.

2. Any such disputes which cannot be settled by negotiations shall be resolved by conciliation or submitted to arbitration.

Article VIII

The Parties agree to establish a claims commission for the mutual settlement of all financial claims.

Article IX

1. This Treaty shall enter into force upon exchange of instruments of ratification.

2. This Treaty supersedes the Agreement between Egypt and Israel of September, 1975.

3. All protocols, annexes, and maps attached to this Treaty shall be regarded as an integral part hereof.

4. The Treaty shall be communicated to the Secretary General of the United Nations for registration in accordance with the provisions of Article 102 of the Charter of the United Nations.

**Author's Note: In addition to the main body of the agreement indicated above, there is also an Annex, an Appendix to the Annex, Agreed Minutes, and an exchange of letters between the leaders that further delineate and clarify various aspects of the peace treaty.

APPENDIX C

*Annual State of the Union Message
(1980) (the Carter Doctrine)*

This last few months has not been an easy time for any of us. As we meet tonight, it has never been more clear that the state of our Union depends on the state of the world. And tonight, as throughout our own generation, freedom and peace in the world depend on the state of our Union.

The 1980's have been born in turmoil, strife, and change. This is a time of challenge to our interests and our values and it's a time that tests our wisdom and our skills.

At this time in Iran, 50 Americans are still held captive, innocent victims of terrorism and anarchy. Also at this moment, massive Soviet troops are attempting to subjugate the fiercely independent and deeply religious people of Afghanistan. These two acts—one of international terrorism and one of military aggression—present a serious challenge to the United States of America and indeed to all the nations of the world. Together, we will meet these threats to peace.

I'm determined that the United States will remain the strongest of all nations, but our power will never be used to initiate a threat to the security of any nation or to the rights of any human being. We seek to be and to remain secure—a nation at peace in a stable world. But to be secure we must face the world as it is.

Three basic developments have helped to shape our challenges: the steady growth and increased projection of Soviet military power beyond its own borders; the overwhelming dependence of the Western democracies on oil supplies from the Middle East; and the press of social and religious and economic and political change in the many nations of the developing world, exemplified by the revolution in Iran.

Each of these factors is important in its own right. Each interacts with the others. All must be faced together, squarely and courageously. We will face these challenges, and we will meet them with the best that is in us. And we will not fail.

In response to the abhorrent act in Iran, our Nation has never been aroused and unified so greatly in peacetime. Our position is clear. The United States will not yield to blackmail.

We continue to pursue these specific goals: first, to protect the present and long-range interests of the United States; secondly, to preserve the lives of the American hostages and to secure, as quickly as possible, their safe release, if possible, to avoid bloodshed which might further endanger the lives of our fellow citizens; to enlist the help of other nations in condemning this act of violence, which is shocking and violates the moral and the legal standards of a civilized world; and also to convince and to persuade the Iranian leaders that the real danger to their nation lies in the north, in the Soviet Union and from the Soviet troops now in Afghanistan, and that the unwarranted Iranian quarrel with the United States hampers their response to this far greater danger to them.

If the American hostages are harmed, a severe price will be paid. We will never rest until every one of the American hostages are released.

But now we face a broader and more fundamental challenge in this region because of the recent military action of the Soviet Union.

Now, as during the last 3 1/2 decades, the relationship between our country, the United States of America, and the Soviet Union is the most critical factor in determining whether the world will live at peace or be engulfed in global conflict.

Since the end of the Second World War, America has led other nations in meeting the challenge of mounting Soviet power. This has not been a simple or a static relationship. Between us there has been cooperation, there has been competition, and at times there has been confrontation.

In the 1940s we took the lead in creating the Atlantic Alliance in response to the Soviet Union's suppression and then consolidation of its East European empire and the resulting threat of the Warsaw Pact to Western Europe.

In the 1950s we helped to contain further Soviet challenges in Korea and in the Middle East, and we rearmed to assure the continuation of that containment.

In the 1960s we met the Soviet challenges in Berlin, and we faced the SALT I and SALT II. Especially now, in a time of great tension, observing the mutual constraints imposed by the terms of these treaties will be in the best interest of both countries and will help to preserve world peace. I will consult very closely with the Congress on this matter as we strive to control nuclear weapons. That effort to control nuclear weapons will not be abandoned.

We superpowers also have the responsibility to exercise restraint in the use of our great military force. The integrity and the independence of weaker nations must not be threatened. They must know that in our presence they are secure.

But now the Soviet Union has taken a radical and an aggressive new step. It's using its great military power against a relatively defenseless nation. The implications of the Soviet invasion of Afghanistan could pose the most serious threat to the peace since the Second World War.

The vast majority of nations on Earth have condemned this latest Soviet attempt to extend its colonial domination of others and have demanded the immediate withdrawal of Soviet troops. The Moslem world is especially and justifiably outraged by this aggression against an Islamic people. No action of a world power has ever been so quickly and so overwhelmingly condemned. But verbal condemnation is not enough. The Soviet Union must pay a concrete price for their aggression.

While this invasion continues, we and the other nations of the world cannot conduct business as usual with the Soviet Union. That's why the United States has imposed stiff economic penalties on the Soviet Union. I will not issue any permits for Soviet ships to fish in the coastal waters of the United States. I've cut Soviet access to high-technology equipment and to agricultural products. I've limited other commerce with the Soviet Union, and I've asked our allies and friends to join with us in restraining their own trade with the Soviets and not to replace our own embargoed items. And I have notified the Olympic

Committee that with Soviet invading forces in Afghanistan, neither the American people nor I will support sending an Olympic team to Moscow.

The Soviet Union is going to have to answer some basic questions: Will it help promote a more stable international environment in which its own legitimate, peaceful concerns can be pursued? Or will it continue to expand its military power far beyond its genuine security needs, and use that power for colonial conquest? The Soviet Union must realize that its decision to use military force in Afghanistan will be costly to every political and economic relationship it values.

The region which is now threatened by Soviet troops in Afghanistan is of great strategic importance: It contains more than two-thirds of the world's exportable oil. The Soviet effort to dominate Afghanistan has brought Soviet military forces to within 300 miles of the Indian Ocean and close to the Straits of Hormuz, a waterway through which most of the world's oil must flow. The Soviet Union is now attempting to consolidate a strategic position, therefore, that poses a grave threat to the free movement of Middle East oil.

This situation demands careful thought, steady nerves, and resolute action, not only for this year but for many years to come. It demands collective efforts to meet this new threat to security in the Persian Gulf and in Southwest Asia. It demands the participation of all those who rely on oil from the Middle East and who are concerned with global peace and stability. And it demands consultation and close cooperation with countries in the area which might be threatened.

Meeting this challenge will take national will, diplomatic and political wisdom, economic sacrifice, and, of course, military capability. We must call on the best that is in us to preserve the security of this crucial region.

Let our position be absolutely clear: An attempt by any outside force to gain control of the Persian Gulf region will be regarded as an assault on the vital interests of the United States of America, and such an assault will be repelled by any means necessary, including military force.

During the past 3 years, you have joined with me to improve our own security and the prospects for peace, not only in the vital oil-producing area of the Persian Gulf region but around the world. We've increased annually our real commitment for defense, and we will sustain this increase of effort throughout the Five Year Defense Program. It's imperative that Congress approve this strong defense budget for 1981, encompassing a 5-percent real growth in authorizations, without any reduction.

We are also improving our capability to deploy U.S. military forces rapidly to distant areas. We've helped to strengthen NATO and our other alliances, and recently we and other NATO members have decided to develop and to deploy modernized, intermediate-range nuclear forces to meet an unwarranted and increased threat from the nuclear weapons of the Soviet Union.

We are working with our allies to prevent conflict in the Middle East. The peace treaty between Egypt and Israel is a notable achievement which represents a strategic asset for America and which also enhances prospects for regional and world peace. We are now engaged in further negotiations to provide full autonomy for the people of the West Bank and Gaza, to resolve the Palestinian issue in all its aspects, and to preserve the peace and security of Israel. Let no one doubt our commitment to the security of Israel. In a few days we will observe an historic event when Israel makes another major withdrawal from the Sinai and when Ambassadors will be exchanged between Israel and Egypt.

We've also expanded our own sphere of friendship. Our deep commitment to human rights and to meeting human needs has improved our relationship with much of the Third World. Our decision to normalize relations with the People's Republic of China will help to preserve peace and stability in Asia and in the Western Pacific.

We've increased and strengthened our naval presence in the Indian Ocean, and we are now making arrangements for key naval and air facilities to be used by our forces in the region of northeast Africa and the Persian Gulf.

We've reconfirmed our 1959 agreement to help Pakistan preserve its independence and its integrity. The United States will take action consistent with our own laws to assist Pakistan in resisting any outside aggression. And I'm asking the Congress specifically to reaffirm this agreement. I'm also working, along with the leaders of other nations, to provide additional military and economic aid for Pakistan. That request will come to you in just a few days.

Finally, we are prepared to work with other countries in the region to share a cooperative security framework that respects differing values and political beliefs, yet which enhances the independence, security, and prosperity of all.

All these efforts combined emphasize our dedication to defend and preserve the vital interests of the region and of the nation which we represent and those of our allies—in Europe and the Pacific, and also in the parts of the world which have such great strategic importance to us, stretching especially through the Middle East and Southwest Asia. With your help, I will pursue these efforts with vigor and with determination. You and I will act as necessary to protect and to preserve our Nation's security.

The men and women of America's Armed Forces are on duty tonight in many parts of the world. I'm proud of the job they are doing, and I know you share that pride. I believe that our volunteer forces are adequate for current defense needs, and I hope that it will not become necessary to impose a draft. However, we must be prepared for that possibility. For this reason, I have determined that the Selective Service System must now be revitalized. I will send legislation and budget proposals to the Congress next month so that we can begin registration and then meet future mobilization needs rapidly if they arise.

We also need clear and quick passage of a new charter to define the legal authority and accountability of our intelligence agencies. We will guarantee that abuses do not recur, but we must tighten our controls on sensitive intelligence information, and we need to remove unwarranted restraints on America's ability to collect intelligence.

The decade ahead will be a time of rapid change, as nations everywhere seek to deal with new problems and age-old tensions. But America need have no fear. We can thrive in a world of change if we remain true to our values and actively engaged in promoting world peace. We will continue to work as we have for peace in the Middle East and southern Africa. We will continue to build our ties with developing nations, respecting and helping to strengthen their national independence which they have struggled so hard to achieve. And we will continue to support the growth of democracy and the protection of human rights.

In repressive regimes, popular frustrations often have no outlet except through violence. But when peoples and their governments can approach their problems together through open, democratic methods, the basis for stability and peace is far more solid and far more enduring. That is why our support for human rights in other countries is in our own national interest as well as part of our own national character.

Peace—a peace that preserves freedom—remains America's first goal. In the coming years, as a mighty nation we will continue to pursue peace. But to be strong abroad we must be strong at home. And in order to be strong, we must continue to face up to the difficult issues that confront us as a nation today.

The crises in Iran and Afghanistan have dramatized a very important lesson: Our excessive dependence on foreign oil is a clear and present danger to our Nation's security. The need has never been more urgent. At long last, we must have a clear, comprehensive energy policy for the United States.

As you well know, I have been working with the Congress in a concentrated and persistent way over the past 3 years to meet this need. We have made progress together. But Congress must act promptly now to complete final action on this vital energy legislation. Our Nation will then have a major conservation effort, important initiatives to develop solar power, realistic pricing based on the true value of oil, strong incentives for the production of coal and other fossil fuels in the United States, and our Nation's most massive peacetime investment in the development of synthetic fuels.

The American people are making progress in energy conservation. Last year we reduced overall petroleum consumption by 8 percent and gasoline consumption by 5 percent below what it was the year before. Now we must do more.

After consultation with the Governors, we will set gasoline conservation goals for each of the 50 States, and I will make them mandatory if these goals are not met.

I've established an import ceiling for 1980 of 8.2 million barrels a day—well below the level of foreign oil purchases in 1977. I expect our imports to be much lower than this, but the ceiling will be enforced by an oil import fee if necessary. I'm prepared to lower these imports still further if the other oil-consuming countries will join us in a fair and mutual reduction. If we have a serious shortage, I will not hesitate to impose mandatory gasoline rationing immediately.

The single biggest factor in the inflation rate last year, the increase in the inflation rate last year, was from one cause: the skyrocketing prices of OPEC oil. We must take whatever actions are necessary to reduce our dependence on foreign oil—and at the same time reduce inflation.

As individuals and as families, few of us can produce energy by ourselves. But all of us can conserve energy—every one of us, every day of our lives. Tonight I call on you—in fact, all the people of America—to help our Nation. Conserve energy. Eliminate waste. Make 1980 indeed a year of energy conservation.

Of course, we must take other actions to strengthen our Nation's economy.

First, we will continue to reduce the deficit and then to balance the Federal budget.

Second, as we continue to work with business to hold down prices, we'll build also on the historic national accord with organized labor to restrain pay increases in a fair fight against inflation.

Third, we will continue our successful efforts to cut paperwork and to dismantle unnecessary Government regulation.

Fourth, we will continue our progress in providing jobs for America, concentrating on a major new program to provide training and work for our young people, especially minority youth. It has been said that "a mind is a terrible thing to waste." We will give our young people new hope for jobs and a better life in the 1980's.

And fifth, we must use the decade of the 1980's to attack the basic structural weaknesses and problems in our economy through measures to increase productivity, savings, and investment.

With these energy and economic policies, we will make America even stronger at home in this decade—just as our foreign and defense policies will make us stronger and safer throughout the world. We will never abandon our struggle for a just and a decent society here at home. That's the heart of America—and it's the source of our ability to inspire other people to defend their own rights abroad.

Our material resources, great as they are, are limited. Our problems are too complex for simple slogans or for quick solutions. We cannot solve them without effort and sacrifice. Walter Lippmann once reminded us, "You took the good things for granted. Now you must earn them again. For every right that you cherish, you have a duty which you must fulfill. For every good which you wish to preserve, you will have to sacrifice your comfort and your ease. There is nothing for nothing any longer."

Our challenges are formidable. But there's a new spirit of unity and resolve in our country. We move into the 1980's with confidence and hope and a bright vision of the America we want: an America strong and free, an America at peace, an America with equal rights for all citizens—and for women, guaranteed in the United States Constitution—an America with jobs and good health and good education for every citizen, an America with a clean and bountiful life in our cities and on our farms, an America that helps to feed the world, an America secure in filling its own energy needs, an America of justice, tolerance, and compassion. For this vision to come true, we must sacrifice, but this national commitment will be an exciting enterprise that will unify our people.

Together as one people, let us work to build our strength at home, and together as one indivisible union, let us seek peace and security throughout the world.

Together let us make of this time of challenge and danger a decade of national resolve and of brave achievement.

Thank you very much.

NOTES

Preface

1. Ray Huang, *1587, A Year of No Significance: The Ming Dynasty in Decline* (New Haven: Yale University Press, 1981).
2. Along with the courses and counsel of two wonderful academic advisers and scholars who have each left their own indelible marks in the field: Lou Cantori and Bob Freedman.

Chapter 1

1. See, for example, Arthur Goldschmidt Jr., *A Concise History of the Middle East* (Boulder: Westview Press, 1991); Peter Mansfield, *A History of the Middle East* (New York: Penguin Books, 1991); Albert Hourani, *A History of the Arab Peoples* (New York: Warner Books, 1991); M. E. Yapp, *The Near East Since the First World War* (London: Longman Group, 1991); Congressional Quarterly, *The Middle East*, 9th ed. (Washington, D.C.: CQ Press, 2000); William B. Quandt, *Peace Process* (Berkeley: University of California Press, 1993); Charles D. Smith, *Palestine and the Arab-Israeli Conflict*, 4th ed. (New York: St. Martin's, 2001); Glenn E. Perry, *The Middle East: Fourteen Islamic Centuries* (Upper Saddle River, N.J.: Prentice Hall, 1997); William L. Cleveland, *A History of the Modern Middle East* (Boulder: Westview Press, 1994); Fred J. Khouri, *The Arab-Israeli Dilemma*, 3rd ed. (Syracuse: Syracuse University Press, 1985); Nadav Safran, *Israel, the Embattled Ally* (Cambridge: Belknap Press of Harvard University Press, 1981); Alan R. Taylor, *The Arab Balance of Power* (Syracuse: Syracuse University Press, 1982); and Walter Laqueur and Barry Rubin, *The Israel-Arab Reader* (New York: Penguin Books, 1991).This type of demarcation is even more prevalent in the broader treatments of Middle East history in world history and Western civilization course texts; for example, see William J. Duker and Jackson J. Spielvogel, *World History*, vol. 2, *Since 1500* (New York: West Publishing, 1994); Richard Goff et al., *The Twentieth Century: A Brief Global History*, 4th ed. (New York: McGraw-Hill, 1994); Stanley Chodorow et al., *A History of the World*, vol. 2

(New York: Harcourt Brace Jovanovich, 1986); and T. Walter Wallbank et al., *Civilization Past and Present*, 6th ed. (Glenview, Ill.: Scott, Foresman, 1987).To my knowledge, the only studies that have explicated the 1979 period (not necessarily the year in and of itself) as a watershed for the entire region are those by Robert O. Freedman, particularly the deservedly well-received following works: Freedman, ed., *The Middle East Since Camp David* (Boulder: Westview Press, 1984); Freedman, *Soviet Policy Toward the Middle East Since 1970*, 3rd ed. (New York: Praeger, 1982); and Freedman, ed., *Moscow and the Middle East: Soviet Policy Since the Invasion of Afghanistan* (Cambridge: Cambridge University Press, 1991). However, *The Middle East After Camp David* is limited in that it was published in 1984; the manuscript was processed prior to the June 1982 Israeli invasion of Lebanon, when the full implications of the 1979 period were only beginning to emerge. The latest edition of *Soviet Policy Toward the Middle East Since 1970* was also published in 1982 and is limited within this context for the same reason. *Moscow and the Middle East: Soviet Policy Since the Invasion of Afghanistan*, published in 1991, focuses primarily on the effects of the invasion on Soviet domestic politics, Soviet foreign policy, and the Soviet position in the Middle East, and in this way is quite useful. However, it is limited to only one of the three primary events of 1979 and remains, for the most part, within the analytical sphere of the Soviet Union. It is also my contention that it is important to use the actual signing of the treaty in 1979, and not the Camp David accords in 1978, as the true breaking point in the process.

2. One notable exception is Ray Huang's *1587, A Year of No Significance: The Ming Dynasty in Decline* (New Haven: Yale University Press, 1981).

3. Indeed, if my calculations are correct, the time period according to the Islamic calendar that would have coincided with 1979 would have been A.H. 1399–1400 (A.H. standing for "anno Hegirae," or the year of the *hijra*, the Prophet Muhammad's emigration from Mecca to Medina in 622 C.E.). The breaking point would have been sometime in the early part of November 1979, so that the Iranian revolution, the Egyptian-Israeli peace treaty, and the taking of the American hostages in Teheran would have been included in one year (A.H. 1399), and the storming of the Grand Mosque in Mecca (November 20, 1979) and the Soviet invasion of Afghanistan in December 1979 would have been included in another year (A.H. 1400). Had I used the Islamic calendar, the title of this book would therefore be *A.H. 1399–1400*!

4. Along this line of thought, there are two recent books that examine the nature of historical counterfactuals, that is, those "what if's" regarding potential historical time lines based on different decisions, whims, and/or chance circumstances at crucial points of history: Niall Ferguson, ed., *Virtual History: Alternatives and Counterfactuals* (New York: Basic Books, 1999); and Robert Cowley, ed., *What If? The World's Foremost Military Historians Imagine What Might Have Been* (New York: G. P. Putnam's Sons, 1999).

5. James Cameron, *1914* (Westport, Conn.: Greenwood Press, 1959), pp. v–vi.

6. Lyn Macdonald, *1915: The Death of Innocence* (New York: Henry Holt, 1993), p. ix.

7. Lyn Macdonald, *1914* (New York: Atheneum, 1988), p. xii.

8. Virginia Cowles, *1913: An End and a Beginning* (New York: Harper & Row, 1967).

9. Immanuel Geiss, ed., *July 1914: The Outbreak of the First World War* (New York: W. W. Norton, 1967).

10. Emil Ludwig, *July '14* (New York: G. P. Putnam's Sons, 1929), p. 16.

11. Gordon Brook-Shepherd, *November 1918* (Boston: Little, Brown, 1981), pp. 9–11.

12. Richard Collier, *1940: The Avalanche* (New York: Dial Press, 1979).

13. William K. Klingaman, *1941: Our Lives in a World on the Edge* (New York: Harper & Row, 1988), p. 463.

14. Thomas Fleming, *1776: Year of Illusions* (New York: W. W. Norton, 1975), p. 479.

15. Tom Segev (English language editor: Arlen Neal Weinstein), *1949: The First Israelis* (New York: Free Press, 1986).

16. Jean Starobinski, *1789: The Emblems of Reason* (Cambridge: MIT Press, 1988), p. 1.

17. James Chandler, *England in 1819: The Politics of Literary Culture and the Case of Romantic Historicism* (Chicago: University of Chicago Press, 1998).

18. Chandler, *England in 1819*, p. 5.

19. John Brewer, "The Year of Writing Dangerously," *New Republic*, August 3, 1998, p. 43.

20. See, for instance, a series of conferences held at the University of Essex, the proceedings of which were published: Francis Barker et al., eds., *1848: The Sociology of Literature, Proceedings of the Essex Conference on the Sociology of Literature* (Colchester: University of Essex, 1978); *1936: The Sociology of Literature* (Colchester: University of Essex, 1979); *1642: Literature and Power in the 17th Century* (Colchester: University of Essex, 1981); and *1789: Reading, Writing, Revolution* (Colchester: University of Essex, 1982). As Adena Rosmarin remarked, "the discipline of literary studies has taken a turn or, more precisely, a return to history," whereas "the discipline of history has taken a turn or, again more precisely, a return to narrative." Adena Rosmarin, "The Narrativity of Interpretive History," in *Reading Narrative: Form, Ethics, Ideology*, ed. James Phelan (Columbus: Ohio State University Press, 1989), p. 12. I am grateful to James Chandler and other literary historians (Hayden White's criticisms notwithstanding) who have blazed a trail and allowed me to elevate my thought processes to a level of methodological introspection that I otherwise would probably not have approached without this cross-disciplinary pollination.

21. Claude Levi-Strauss, *The Savage Mind* (Chicago: University of Chicago Press, 1966).

22. See Jean-Paul Sartre, *Search for Method* (New York: Knopf, 1963).

23. Levi-Strauss, *The Savage Mind*, p. 258. Chandler also comments on this subject; see Chandler, *England in 1819*, pp. 65–79.

24. Chandler, *England in 1819*, p. 67.

25. Levi-Strauss, *The Savage Mind*, p. 259.

26. Robert Gilpin, *War and Change in World Politics* (Cambridge: Cambridge University Press, 1981), p. 11.

27. Levi-Strauss, *The Savage Mind*, pp. 260–261.

28. Ibid., p. 261.

29. Levi-Strauss, *The Scope of Anthology* (London: Jonathan Cape, 1967), pp. 46–47, as quoted in Chandler, *England in 1819*, p. 68.

30. Levi-Strauss, *The Savage Mind*, p. 259.

31. Ibid., p. 257.

32. I would contend that there exists a legitimate level between that of the annual and secular: the decade. This is justified especially considering the fact that we are operating at no greater level in this book than the secular. It would seem, then, to be an appropriate level of analysis in which the year 1979 would also stand up to scrutiny; that is, it would still be considered a watershed in a level above its own domain.

33. *Webster's New Collegiate Dictionary* (Springfield, Mass.: G. & C. Merriam Company, 1979), p. 392.

34. François Furet, *In the Workshop of History* (Chicago: University of Chicago Press, 1984), p. 55.

35. A more thorough discussion of the return of narrative and the Annales school will follow. For two particularly influential articles on the subject, see Philippe Carrard, "To Tell or Not to Tell: The New History and the Rebirth of Narrative," *French Forum* 14, no. 2 (May 1989); and Lawrence Stone, "The Revival of Narrative: Reflections on a New Old History," *Past and Present* 85 (November 1979).

36. Edgar Morin, "Le Retour de l'événement," *Communications* 18 (1972): 6–20; also, see Carrard, "To Tell or Not to Tell," p. 224.

37. Frederick J. Teggart, *Theory and Processes of History* (Berkeley: University of California Press, 1960), p. 151.

38. Ibid.

39. René Descartes, *Philosophical Works*, translated by E. S. Haldane and G. R. T. Ross, vol. 1 (Cambridge: Cambridge University Press, 1911), pp. 84–85, quoted in Teggart, *Theory and Processes of History*, p. 19.

40. Teggart, *Theory and Processes of History*, p. 35.

41. Peter Munz, *The Shapes of Time: A New Look at the Philosophy of History* (Middletown, Conn.: Wesleyan University Press, 1977), p. 31.

42. Lawrence Brian Lombard, *Events: A Metaphysical Study* (London: Routledge and Kegan Paul, 1986), p. 99.

43. Munz, *The Shapes of Time*, p. 22.

44. Teggart, *Theory and Processes of History*, pp. 143–144.

45. Lombard, *Events: A Metaphysical Study*, pp. 79–110; see also Peter Geach's model in N. Rescher, ed., *The Logic of Decision and Action* (Pittsburgh: University of Pittsburgh Press, 1967), pp. 96–103.

46. Lombard, *Events: A Metaphysical Study*, p. 84.

47. Ibid., pp. 90–91.

48. Gilpin, *War and Change in World Politics*, p. 1.

49. Ibid., p. 3.

50. Ibid., p. 14.

51. Ibid., pp. 39–44.

52. Zeev Maoz, *Domestic Sources of Global Change* (Ann Arbor: University of Michigan Press, 1996), p. 5.

53. Ibid. Maoz uses the example of a change from administration to administration (even many coups d'état) as simple change, whereas a true revolution, where there are fundamental changes in the institutions and rules of "political functioning," is an example of transformation. Maoz, like others, also marks the distinction in terms of evolutionary versus revolutionary change (p. 10).

54. Ibid. This discussion is drawn from pages 12–21.

55. Ibid., p. 21.

56. Lombard, *Events: A Metaphysical Study*, pp. 72–73; he also states that "to be an event is to be a thing having a place as a link in the chain of causes and effects" (p. 73). W. H. Walsh states that the "notion of cause was introduced into history from everyday life, which means that a cause in history was, originally, an event, action, or omission but for which the whole subsequent course of events would have been significantly different." W. H. Walsh, *An Introduction to Philosophy of History* (New Jersey: Humanities Press, 1967), p. 190. G. R. Elton suggests that causes are "those antecedent events, actions, thoughts, and situations which can be proved, by demonstration and inference, to have influenced the coming about of the event which he is trying to explain." G. R. Elton, *Political History: Principles and Practice* (New York: Basic Books, 1970), p. 137. This contrasts with what Michael Oakeshott has said for many years; indeed, he would erase the term "cause" from the historian's lexicon: "The conception of cause is thus replaced by the exhibition of a world of events intrinsically related to one another in which no lacuna is tolerated. To see all the degrees of change is to be in possession of a world of facts which calls for no further explanation. In history, 'pour savoir les choses, il faut savoir le détail.'" Michael Oakeshott, *Experience and Its Modes* (Cambridge: Cambridge University Press, 1933), p. 143; see also Oakeshott's *On History and Other Essays* (Oxford: Basil Blackwell, 1983).

57. Michael Stanford, *Introduction to the Philosophy of History* (Malden, Mass.: Blackwell, 1998), p. 86. See also R. G. Collingwood, *An Essay on Metaphysics* (New York: Clarendon Press, 1940), pp. 296–297; Collingwood states: "A cause is an event or state of things which it is in our power to produce or prevent, and by producing or preventing which we can produce or prevent that whose cause it is said to be."

58. Stanford, *Introduction to the Philosophy of History*, pp. 86–87; also, see Walsh, *An Introduction to Philosophy of History*, p. 191.

59. Elton, *Political History*, p. 138. Elton goes on to state: "All historical events are the products of causes of both types. Direct causes explain why the event actually happened; situational causes explain why direct causes proved effective and why the event occupies a particular place in the historical picture and story, both as an effect and as a cause of further effects" (p. 140).

60. Stanford states that "human affairs are so complex that it may legitimately be doubted whether causes in history can ever be identified completely or accurately related to their effects or (even if not certainly) at least with a

degree of practical and useful probability" (p. 91). Walsh writes that "every factor we add calls for the addition of further co-operating factors, so that we are threatened with having to say that the causes of *any* historical event must be *all* the events which preceded it" (p. 191).

61. Stanford, *Introduction to the Philosophy of History*, p. 86.

62. Walsh, *An Introduction to Philosophy of History*, p. 199.

63. Ibid., p. 198.

64. As will be discussed in the next section of this chapter, historians are reemphasizing the role of individual will, ideas, religion, and culture as significant elements of change rather than solely structural causes, such as demographic or economic factors. This lends a great deal of unpredictability to the exercise, and, thus, general laws are seen as inherently unreliable, something that has been a traditional hallmark of the difference between history and the scientifically oriented disciplines (and between the narrative and Annales modes of history).

65. Stanford, *Introduction to Philosophy of History*, pp. 88–90.

66. Stone, "The Revival of Narrative: Reflections on a New Old History."

67. Philippe Carrard, in his article "To Tell or Not to Tell: The New History and the Rebirth of Narrative," explains how the vigorous antinarrative attitude of the new historians was a product of the need in the early years of the "new history" to distinguish itself against the positivist narrative history that preceded and still dominated the field at the time.

68. On this point, see Jacques Le Goff, "Is Politics Still the Backbone of History?" in *Historical Studies Today*, ed. Felix Gilbert and Stephen R. Graubard (New York: W. W. Norton, 1972), pp. 337–355.

69. Carrard, "To Tell or Not to Tell," p. 220. The primary theoretical text that laid the basis for the Annales school was Fernand Braudel's *La Méditerranée et le monde méditerranéen a l'époque de Philippe II*, published in 1949.

70. Le Roy Ladurie, one of the leaders of the Annales movement, stated, prematurely as it turns out, in 1972 that "present-day historiography, with its preference for the quantifiable, the statistical, and the structural, has been obliged to suppress in order to survive. In the last decades it has virtually condemned to death the narrative history of events and the individual biography." Le Roy Ladurie, *The Territory of the Historian*, trans. Ben and Sian Reynolds (New York: Hassocks Press, 1979), p. 111.

71. François Furet, *In the Workshop of History*, trans. Jonathan Mandelbaum (Chicago: University of Chicago Press, 1984), p. 54. He goes on to state that "in short, narrative history reconstructs an experience along a temporal axis" (p. 56).

72. William C. Dowling, *Jameson, Althusser, Marx: An Introduction to the Political Unconscious* (Ithaca: Cornell University Press, 1984), p. 95. See also Fredric Jameson, *The Political Unconscious: Narrative as a Socially Symbolic Act* (Ithaca: Cornell University Press, 1981).

73. Carrard, "To Tell or Not to Tell," p. 221.

74. As Carrard states, "they [New Historians] kept telling stories, even though these stories were no longer—or not exclusively—chronicles of the

state, but accounts of the origin and development of social structures, economic trends, and cultural attitudes." Ibid.

75. Ibid., p. 222.

76. Furet, *In the Workshop of History*, p. 67.

77. Jean-Pierre V. M. Herubel, *Annales Historiography and Theory: A Selective and Annotated Bibliography* (Westport, Conn.: Greenwood Press, 1994), p. 5. Not willing to concede too much, Le Roy Ladurie would consider this shift in the Annales school as using the study of events to illuminate "the makeup of a structure, not as changing the structure itself" (Carrard, "To Tell or Not to Tell," p. 225).

78. Carrard, "To Tell or Not to Tell," p. 223. As examples of this transformation within the Annales school, Carrard points to Georges Duby's *Le Dimanche de Bouvines* (1973), which is a description of a single battle in 1214, and Le Roy Ladurie's (who has been called one of the radical Annalistes) *Le Carnaval de Romans* (1979), which also looks at a single event, in this case, a carnival in a small town in Dauphine in 1580. On this, see also Stone, "The Revival of Narrative," pp. 17–18; and Philippe Carrard, "Theory and Practice: Historical Enunciation and the Annales School," in *A New Philosophy of History*, ed. Frank Ankersmit and Hans Kellner (Chicago: University of Chicago Press, 1995), p. 112.

79. Stone, "The Revival of Narrative," p. 10.

80. Dowling, *Jameson, Althusser, Marx*, pp. 98–99.

81. Allan Megill, "Grand Narrative and the Discipline of History," in *A New Philosophy of History*, ed. Frank Ankersmit and Hans Kellner (Chicago: University of Chicago Press, 1995), p. 170.

82. Quoted in ibid., p. 173.

83. My thanks to my colleague in the Department of History at Trinity University, John Martin, for suggesting the term "secular priesthood."

Chapter 2

1. Certainly the Iranian episode meets the criteria for a revolution, such as a transfer of power from one class to another and an almost completely altered political system based on a new prevailing ideology; indeed, it is one of the few true revolutions in the twentieth century.

2. Nikki Keddie, *Roots of Revolution: An Interpretive History of Modern Iran* (New Haven: Yale University Press, 1981), pp. 93–112.

3. See Hamid Algar, *Islam and Revolution: Writings and Declarations of Imam Khomeini* (Berkeley: Mizan Press, 1981).

4. The cease-fire that brought an end to the War of Attrition in August 1970, known as the Rogers Initiative (named after U.S. Secretary of State William Rogers) indicated to U.S. policymakers, most importantly Henry Kissinger, that maybe limited, step-by-step agreements between the Arabs and the Israelis were the most that could be hoped for at the time. The limited agreements would build confidence and trust between Arabs and Israelis, which would lead to broader agreements that in the end might result in a compre-

hensive Arab-Israeli peace. Starting out with a comprehensive peace as the immediate objective through the convening of an international conference (as was envisioned with the Rogers Plan promulgated in late 1969) proved to be unsuccessful because of the complicated and untenable issues that prevented any peace process from getting off the ground. Progress needed to made first on less contentious items where there existed some mutual interest. Kissinger would employ this step-by-step approach at the end of the 1973 Arab-Israeli war.

5. The fourth revenue-producer was (and remains) remittances from Egyptians working abroad, at the time primarily as laborers in the oil-rich countries of the Gulf and in professional positions throughout the Arab world.

6. 'Asad refused to commit the Syrian air force because of his fear that this would be the tripwire for an Israeli military response, and he was probably correct. This breach between 'Asad and the Syrian leader at the time, Salah Jadid, was a prelude to the November 1970 coup that brought Hafiz al-'Asad to power as president of Syria.

7. The PLO then moved to Beirut, where it again soon became something of a state within a state, contributing to the upsetting of the tenuous balances of forces in Lebanon, which led to the 1975–1976 civil war and the Israeli invasion of Lebanon in 1982.

8. In reality, only the Arab members of OPEC (OAPEC or the Organization of Arab Petroleum Exporting Countries) were involved in the strategic plans concerning an oil embargo, primarily to prevent a U.S. ally and OPEC member, such as Iran, from divulging the operations and to better ensure unity of purpose.

9. This caught Syrian President Hafiz al-'Asad off guard as well. He was led to believe that Sadat shared his own more grandiose objectives of at least regaining the territories lost in the 1967 conflagration, which in Syria's case meant the Golan Heights. On the battlefield, Sadat's strategy translated into Egypt's reluctance to advance from the position it had gained on the east bank of the Suez Canal, especially in a reluctance to leave its air defense umbrella. This enabled Israel to focus more of its attention in beating back the Syrians in the north. Sadat, under pressure from the Syrians as well as the Soviets, finally did order his troops to break out from their static position and launched an offensive against Israel, which was followed by a successful Israeli counteroffensive; Israeli troops eventually recrossed the Suez Canal and surrounded the Egyptian Third Army at Suez City toward the latter stages of the conflict. However, 'Asad never forgave Sadat for not fully informing him of the Egyptian president's hidden agenda.

10. For more on Kissinger's wartime and postwar diplomacy, see Nadav Safran's *Israel: The Embattled Ally* (Cambridge: Belknap Press of Harvard University Press, 1982).

11. Israeli and Egyptian forces withdrew from their confrontational position in the Sinai Peninsula and in Suez City on the west bank of the canal. Formally called the "Disengagement of Forces Agreement," it provided for the final withdrawal of Israeli troops from the west side of the canal and mapped out the zones in which Egyptian forces could be stationed on the east side of

the canal. A disengagement agreement between Syria and Israel regarding the separation of forces in the Golan Heights was also negotiated by Kissinger and was consummated in May 1974.

12. On the Brookings Institution report, see William B. Quandt, *Decade of Decisions: American Policy Toward the Arab-Israeli Conflict, 1967–1976* (Berkeley: University of California Press, 1977), pp. 290–291. Several of the members of the study group that assembled the report joined the foreign policymaking apparatus of the Carter administration, including Quandt and, most particularly, Zbigniew Brzezinski, who would become President Carter's national security advisor.

13. As the Israeli defense minister at the time, Ezer Weizman, blatantly observed, Begin saw the Sadat initiative as a golden opportunity to "use every ruse to sabotage the peace efforts leading to Geneva and to promote Israel's long-standing goal of separating Egypt from the other Arab states as a means of weakening Arab bargaining power and making it easier for Israel to hold onto to the remainder of the occupied territories and to ignore the Palestinian problem."

14. One impasse was the Israeli "sweep" of southern Lebanon in June 1978 to root out PLO strongholds that had been launching attacks into northern Israel. It was very embarrassing for Sadat to be engaged in peace negotiations with Israel while the latter was essentially invading another Arab country.

15. Quoted in Thomas T. Hammond, *Red Flag over Afghanistan: The Communist Coup, the Soviet Invasion, and the Consequences* (Boulder: Westview Press, 1984), p. 7.

16. Ibid., p. 5.

17. Moscow began to increase its military support of and influence in Afghanistan in the 1950s in reaction to the cold war–inspired Baghdad Pact formed in 1955, a pro-West defense alliance aimed at containing Soviet expansion that initially included Turkey, Iran, Pakistan, Iraq, and Great Britain. The United States supported the Baghdad Pact but initially assumed only an observer status so as not to disrupt its interests with regard to the Arab states and the Arab-Israeli arena; it later joined the pact outright after the Iraqi revolution in 1958 removed Baghdad from the alliance, thereafter renamed the Central Treaty Organization, or CENTO.

18. See Anthony Arnold, *Afghanistan: The Soviet Invasion in Perspective* (Stanford: Hoover Institution Press, 1985), p. 58.

19. Hammond, *Red Flag over Afghanistan*, p. 39. Most of the aid was never delivered, and the Iranian revolution that ousted the Shah in February 1979 obviated the economic aid program.

20. Ibid., p. 41.

21. Hammond, *Red Flag over Afghanistan*, p. 49; and Arnold, *Afghanistan: The Soviet Invasion in Perspective*, p. 65.

22. Hammond, *Red Flag over Afghanistan*, p. 69.

23. Olivier Roy, *Islam and Resistance in Afghanistan* (New York: Cambridge University Press, 1990), pp. 10, 95–97.

24. Roy suggests that the urgency felt by the new regime to implement these far-reaching reforms stems from its reading of Afghani history, when

King Amanullah attempted in the 1920s to implement a wide-ranging modernization program, emulating both Ataturk and Reza Shah, only to encounter opposition from traditional elements of society, which resulted in his overthrow in 1928. The new regime believed it had to act fast in order to restructure society before allowing any opposition to incrementally build up. Roy, *Islam and Resistance in Afghanistan*, p. 84. Roy further states: "The goal was clear: to cause the old Afghanistan to disappear, by dissolving the social structures and uprooting them from the memory of the whole people, by striking down middle-class people of influence (rather than the aristocracy, considered to be less dangerous because it was cut off from the people), the ulama, guardians of the age-old Islamic culture, and finally young non-Marxist intellectuals, who might have shown a different way towards modernity." Roy, *Islam and Resistance in Afghanistan*, p. 97.

25. However, Islamist opposition to central authority was apparent as early as 1975 against the Daoud regime. M. Hassan Kakar, *Afghanistan: The Soviet Invasion and the Afghan Response, 1979–1982* (Berkeley: University of California Press, 1995), p. 13.

26. Kakar states, however, that Amin was elevated to the position of First Minister *(Lomray Wazir)* and not formally to prime minister as is popularly accepted. Kakar, *Afghanistan: The Soviet Invasion and the Afghan Response*, p. 35.

27. There were approximately 4,500 Soviet military advisors in Afghanistan by November 1979, and Soviet pilots were already flying jet fighters and helicopter gunships against the rebel forces. Ibid., p. 75.

28. Adding to suspicions that Amin was on the CIA payroll was the fact that he had twice been to the United States on educational grants and had obtained a master's degree from Columbia University. In fact, he was preparing to begin his doctoral dissertation when he was summoned to Afghanistan in 1965, reportedly extremely disgruntled that he was forced to give up his studies.

29. Arnold, *Afghanistan: The Soviet Invasion in Perspective*, p. 86.

30. The official request went as follows: "Because of the continuation and expansion of aggression, intervention, and provocations by the foreign enemies of Afghanistan and for the purpose of defending the gains of the Saur Revolution, territorial integrity, national independence, and the preservation of peace and security, and on the basis of the treaty of friendship, good-neighborliness, and cooperation dated 5 December 1978, the Democratic Republic of Afghanistan earnestly demands that the USSR render urgent political, moral, and economic assistance, including military aid, to Afghanistan" (quoted in Hammond, *Red Flag over Afghanistan*, p. 100).

31. Kakar and others assert that, in fact, Amin was in fairly good control of the country, since he had assumed most of the reins of power, and that the Islamist opposition really did not coalesce into a bona fide threat until *after* the Soviet invasion. It follows, then, that one of the main reasons for the invasion was the fact that Amin had shown himself not to be a pliable tool of the Kremlin and had fended off covert Soviet efforts to displace him. Indeed, Kakar sees most explanations as ex post facto Kremlin rationalizations that cover up

the real reason for the invasion: imperialist expansion. See Kakar, *Afghanistan: The Soviet Invasion and the Afghan Response,* pp. 46–50.

32. Arnold argues that the Brezhnev Doctrine does not apply in this case because the Soviet Union made a concerted attempt from mid-1979 on to eliminate the word "socialist" from the Soviet lexicon regarding Afghanistan. In addition, the Kremlin emphasized after the invasion that Afghanistan was in its "national democratic" phase of development and had not yet evolved into a full-fledged communist state. Arnold goes on to surmise that this might have been purposeful in order to eliminate at least any ideological barriers to withdrawal if it became necessary to do so. Arnold, *Afghanistan: The Soviet Invasion in Perspective,* pp. 90–91 and 133–134.

33. On the other hand, many American analysts assumed the U.S.S.R. had learned the lesson we so painfully learned in Vietnam and figured that Moscow would know better than to do something similar in Afghanistan. In addition, many Carter administration officials simply could not believe that the Soviets would risk the SALT II agreement and what was left of détente. On the other hand, the feeling that détente had been unraveling anyway may have convinced some in the Kremlin that there was not much to lose.

Chapter 3

1. We already have an example in the Middle East of this type of changed historical categorization: the Lebanese civil war. When I was studying the Middle East in the late 1970s and early 1980s, when one referred to the Lebanese civil war, it pertained specifically to the years 1975–1976, enveloping primarily the Syrian role in the conflict largely precipitated by the entrance of the PLO after the latter was expelled from Jordan in the 1970 Jordanian civil war, also known as Black September. However, as the disastrous repercussions of the Israeli invasion of Lebanon in 1982 became apparent, and as the Israeli occupation of southern Lebanon continued amid harassment by Hizbullah and the continued deterioration of Lebanese society into the late 1980s, officials and scholars alike began referring to the Lebanese civil war as lasting from 1975 to 1991, when the al-Ta'if accords negotiated in 1989 finally went into effect. The period between 1976 and 1982 is now seen as just a brief interlude (save for the 1978 Israeli sweep of southern Lebanon that presaged their more ambitious venture in 1982) in a single historical event.

2. Mahmood Sariolghalam, "Conceptual Sources of Post-Revolutionary Iranian Behaviour Toward the Arab World," in *Iran and the Arab World,* ed. Hooshang Amirahmadi and Nader Entessar (New York: St. Martin's Press, 1993), p. 22. Khomeini remarked in 1981 that "Palestine and Lebanon have been our primary concern, and have never been separate from our concerns in Iran. In general, a Muslim should not just concern himself with only a group of Muslims. We are all responsible to stand up to the oppression by the superpowers and discredit plans like those of Sadat and [Saudi King] Fahd." Quoted in ibid., p. 23.

3. It should be noted, however, that although it is my opinion (as well as many others) that the Iranian revolution at least to some degree stimulated like action elsewhere in the Middle East, such as the Mecca incident, the extent to which Khomeinism actually appealed to Sunnis is debatable. Indeed, some contend that it drove the wedge between Sunnis and Shiites deeper, despite the attempts by the regime in Teheran to attract and inspire Sunni movements. As Olivier Roy writes: "The dominance of Shiism prevents Iran from laying claim to overall Islamic radicalism, for the Sunnis cannot identify with it. The virulent activism of the Muslim Brotherhood and the Wahhabis [and the Taliban] is openly anti-Shiite (and vice versa). Iran's revolutionary influence extended to Shiism and not to Islamic radicalism." Olivier Roy, *The Failure of Political Islam* (Cambridge: Harvard University Press, 1994), p. 191.

4. William B. Quandt, *Saudi Arabia in the 1980s: Foreign Policy, Security, and Oil* (Washington, D.C.: Brookings Institution, 1981), p. 94.

5. Interior Minister Prince Nayif stated in January 1980 that 127 Saudi soldiers had been killed as a result of the siege at the Grand Mosque, while 75 of the infiltrators also died. The French provided "modest assistance" to the Saudis during the incident; the French had been providing the Saudi security forces with various types of assistance, including counterterrorist training. Quandt, *Saudi Arabia in the 1980s*, p. 83.

6. Saddam also digested 500 Shiite demonstrators in Bahrain in August 1979 calling for the release of one of their religious leaders and the establishment of an Islamic state. As mentioned in the text, Bahrain, like Iraq, consisted of a majority Shiite population ruled by a Sunni minority.

7. Chronology, *Middle East Journal* 33, no. 3 (Autumn 1979): 487.

8. Saudi Arabia's King Fahd asserted that prior to Iraq's attack on Iran in 1980, Saddam Hussein told him, "It is more useful to hit them [the Iranians] now because they are weak. If we leave them until they become strong, they will overrun us." See text of interview with King Fahd in London's *al-Hawadith, Foreign Broadcast Information Service: Near East and South Asia,* February 14, 1992, p. 21. (My thanks to Steve Yetiv at Old Dominion University for finding this quote for me).

9. The Carter administration nonetheless initiated contacts with the Khomeini regime, hoping to open up a dialogue and possibly some sort of a relationship. The administration had no illusions about recreating anything close to the relationship Washington had built up with the Shah, but since the new Islamic Republic was also vehemently anticommunist (and therefore not inclined to pursue relations with the Soviet Union), it was felt that a modus vivendi of sorts might be attainable.

10. For more on this episode, see Gary Sick, *All Fall Down: America's Tragic Encounter with Iran* (New York: Penguin Books, 1986), pp. 329–356.

11. For more on the makeup of the various factions in the Iranian revolution, see Nikki R. Keddie, *Roots of Revolution: An Interpretive History of Modern Iran* (New Haven: Yale University Press, 1981).

12. By December it was clear that Iran had targeted Lebanon, with its Shiite majority, as a prime area of ingress into the heartland of the Middle East and smack into the Arab-Israeli conflict. It was reported on December 10, 1979,

that "Lebanon closed its airspace to Iranian planes in order to prevent Iranian 'volunteers' from entering the country to fight against Israel alongside Palestinian guerrillas" (Chronology, *Middle East Journal* 34, no. 2 [Spring 1980]: 173). On December 19, a second group of Iranian volunteers had arrived in Syria hoping to make their way to Lebanon. (Ibid.) Earlier in the year, in September, Iranian Foreign Minister Ibrahim Yazdi met with President Hafiz al-'Asad in Damascus. In October, Syria hosted another Iranian high-level official, this time Vice Premier Sadiq Tabataba'i. 'Asad then met with Iranian Premier Mehdi Bazargan in Algiers in November. Obviously, Lebanon was a major subject of discussion, and it seems that the foundation for Iranian influence in Lebanon as well as the Iranian-Syrian alliance was being laid.

13. Interestingly, most Shiite Muslims in southern Lebanon at first welcomed the Israeli invasion, since they, too, shared the initial Israeli objective of ridding the area of the PLO. To Shiite Muslims, the PLO had established a state within a state, often treating them with disdain and inviting Israeli reprisals for guerrilla activities that more often than not led to Shiite rather than Palestinian casualties. It was the decision by Israel to stay on in south Lebanon that, in retrospect, was a monumental error and led directly to the radicalization of the Shiite community in Lebanon, which opened the door for both Iranian and Syrian influence.

14. Ironically, the Sandinista regime came to power after overthrowing the U.S.-supported regime of Anastasio Somoza on July 19, 1979.

15. Gary Sick, "The United States in the Persian Gulf: From Twin Pillars to Dual Containment," in *The Middle East and the United States: A Historical and Political Reassessment*, 2nd edition, ed. David W. Lesch (Boulder: Westview Press, 1999), p. 282.

16. This was not the first time an Islamist movement in Egypt attempted to assassinate the Egyptian president. By the end of 1954, the Muslim Brotherhood, which had been allied with revolutionary elements in the overthrow of the monarchy in 1952, had become disillusioned by the secularist Nasserist regime, especially after it signed in October 1954 what the Muslim Brotherhood thought was an inadequate agreement with Britain over British withdrawal from Egypt. In December, MB loyalists tried to assassinate Nasser, and they came very close to doing so. Thereafter, the Nasserist regime arrested, executed, and otherwise repressed MB loyalists, effectively snuffing out the movement until the debacle of 1967, along with the writings of executed Islamist ideologue Sayyid Qutb and the economic dislocation and corruption of the Sadat years, resuscitated the movement in the late 1970s.

17. On the socioeconomic roots of Islamism since the 1970s, see an excellent article by Philip S. Khoury, "Islamic Revivalism and the Crisis of the Secular State in the Arab World: An Historical Appraisal," in *Arab Resources: The Transformation of a Society*, ed. Ibrahim Ibrahim (London: Croom Helm, 1983), pp. 213–234. In the Syrian case, it was an event in 1979 that exponentially raised the level of tension between the government and the Muslim Brotherhood, essentially foreclosing on the possibility of a peaceful resolution of the confrontation. On June 16 Islamists stormed a military academy in Aleppo killing 32 cadets and injuring 54 others. On June 22, Syrian Interior

Minister Adnan Daggagh stated that the government would "liquidate them mercilessly." Three years later at Hama, it did. Chronology, *Middle East Journal* 33, no. 4 (Autumn 1979): 491.

18. See Samuel P. Huntington, *The Clash of Civilizations: Remaking of World Order* (New York: Simon & Schuster, 1996).

19. It is important to note, however, that the Soviet Union did not send any significant military aid to Iraq for about 18 months after the invasion in a show of displeasure toward the Iraqi regime's decision to invade at a time when the Soviets were involved in Afghanistan and in a position to improve relations with Teheran now that the United States was clearly on the outs with the Iranian regime.

20. Inducing this line of thinking were periodic skirmishes between Arabs in Khuzistan and Iranian government troops over the demand for more autonomy. A particularly bloody confrontation occurred in May 1979, when at least 21 people were killed when Arab demonstrators engaged government troops in Khorramshahr. Earlier, in April, representatives from Khuzistan had officially demanded more autonomy for the province. Saddam had obviously taken notice of these events.

21. Although the GCC has made itself into a more formidable trading bloc than its constituent parts could have accomplished on their own, there are those who suggest that regional trade blocs such as this may be counterproductive to overall liberalization and integration into the global market. As Pierre Sauve and Arvind Subramanian state, "The systemic effects of these regional agreements for multilateral bargaining are perverse: countries in a regional arrangement may actually oppose broad-based liberalization in the WTO because their preferential access to each other's main export markets is likely to be eroded." "Weakness at the Heart of World Trade," *Financial Times*, June 7, 2000, p. 17.

22. Rosemarie Said Zahlan, *The Making of the Modern Gulf States* (London: Ithaca Press, 1998), pp. 159–184.

23. The GCC would take this one step further in the aftermath of the 1991 Gulf war. In March 1991, the GCC countries signed an agreement in Damascus with Syria and Egypt that became known as the Damascus Declaration. The new organization, sometimes called the "GCC Plus Two," intended to create an all-Arab security contingent (called the Arab Peacekeeping Force), with Egypt and Syria providing the bulk of the muscle and the GCC providing most of the financial support. Although the Damascus Declaration exists today more in theory than reality, the participants still meet on occasion, which reminds everyone in the region of how inept the Arab League as a whole has been in providing security for its members.

24. See, for instance, Lawrence Freedman and Efraim Karsh, *The Gulf Conflict, 1990–1991: Diplomacy and War in the New World Order* (Princeton: Princeton University Press, 1993); for a shorter treatment on the U.S.-Iraqi relationship that led up to the war, see Amatzia Baram, "U.S. Input into Iraqi Decisionmaking, 1988–1990," in *The Middle East and the United States: A Historical and Political Reassessment*, 2nd ed., ed. David W. Lesch (Boulder: Westview Press, 1999), pp. 313–340; and for an excellent examination of the

decisionmaking process of the Bush administration in going to war to liberate Kuwait, see Steve A. Yetiv's upcoming book, at the present time tentatively titled, *Fateful Decisions: Explaining the Last Major Middle East Crisis of the 20th Century.*

25. There were a number of other Iraqi claims as well, such as accusing the Kuwaitis of purposely exceeding their OPEC oil production quota in order to flood the oil market and drive down the price of oil, which inhibited the ability of Iraq to recover from the war with Iran. Although this may have been a serendipitous result from the Kuwaiti point of view, the primary reason for Kuwaiti overproduction was economic; by 1990, Kuwait actually received more revenue from its investments abroad than from its considerable oil production, investments that would bring a higher return with boisterous economies fueled by low oil prices and subsequent low inflation rates. Saddam Hussein also made the rather spurious claim, as did one of his predecessors, Colonel Abd al-Karim Qassim, in 1961, that Kuwait was an integral part of Iraq; indeed, it was called the nineteenth province of Iraq, based on the fact that Kuwait had been a part of the province of Basra in the Ottoman Empire. The Iraqi president obviously overlooked the fact that, if anything, Iraq is more of an artificial creation than Kuwait, having been pieced together by the victorious Entente powers following the defeat of the Ottoman Empire in World War I.

26. See Amatzia Baram, "U.S. Input into Iraqi Decisionmaking, 1988–1990," in *The Middle East and the United States: A Historical and Political Reassessment,* 2nd ed., ed. David W. Lesch (Boulder: Westview Press, 1999), pp. 313–340.

27. It is important to remember, however, that even if the Bush administration had been so inclined, it would have been difficult, if not counterproductive, to move a deterrent force into the Gulf in an attempt to force Iraq's massing troops to retreat. Washington's allies in the Gulf, including Kuwait and Saudi Arabia, had resumed their arms-length relationship with the United States, preferring to distance themselves for fear of domestic backlash—especially since the U.S. presence in the Gulf had been demonstrably enhanced during the Iran-Iraq war. Gulf leaders, in addition to Egyptian President Hosni Mubarak, who met with Saddam just prior to the invasion, were assuring the Bush administration that Iraq was just saber rattling in order to intimidate Kuwait to make concessions on some of the outstanding issues between them. All the Bush administration could do at the time, in terms of concrete action in the Gulf, was to hold a joint refueling exercise with the UAE.

28. Until that time, most analysts predicted Saddam would remain in Kuwait City and not spring the proverbial trip wire by moving to the Saudi border. Many figured that Iraq would withdraw after securing Kuwaiti concessions, keeping the Rumaylah oil field and offshore islands and possibly damaging or destroying Kuwait's oil production capability in order to drive up the price of oil. Most of the active Saudi oil fields are in the northeast portion of the country nearest to the Kuwaiti border and, therefore, are particularly vulnerable to quick incursion, which is something that actually could have been accomplished before U.S. troops arrived en masse, thus dramatically driving

up the price of oil. Oil was a major factor, of course, in U.S. calculations. Underlining this importance was the fear in the White House that the countries emerging from under the Soviet yoke at the end of the cold war desperately needed a moderate oil price. If the price of oil continued to rise or stay at heightened levels in the aftermath of the Iraqi invasion, it could have severely curtailed the ability of these countries to stabilize themselves economically and survive the break from the Soviet bloc. The oil markets needed the United States to take dramatic action in order to correct the oil price imbalance. Indeed, the day the United States launched Operation Desert Storm, the price of oil dropped.

29. See Yetiv, *Fateful Decisions.*

30. On the pros and cons of "dual containment," see Graham Fuller et al., "Symposium on Dual Containment: U.S. Policy Toward Iran and Iraq," *Middle East Policy* 3, no. 3 (1994): 1–26; Robert S. Deutsch et al., "Symposium: From Containment to Stability," *Middle East Policy* 5, no. 2 (1997): 1–21; and Robert S. Deutsch et al., "Differentiated Containment," *Foreign Affairs* 76, no. 3 (May-June 1997): 20–52.

31. Similar to President Hafiz al-'Asad's decision to support Iran against Iraq, Syria's going against the grain in support of the U.S.-led coalition was not all that illogical when one considers the circumstances. The same differences between Syria and Iraq that compelled Damascus to support Teheran in the Iran-Iraq war still existed. On top of that, with the end of the cold war and the subsequent implosion of the Soviet Union, it was clear that Syria's superpower patron would be unable to provide it with the political, economic, and military support to which it had become accustomed. In a sense, Hafiz al-'Asad's decision to join the coalition was Syria's coming-out party to the West in the hope of gaining more favorable consideration from the European Union in economic terms, build bridges to the United States, acquire much needed aid from what would certainly be a most grateful set of Arab countries in the Gulf, and, as a quid pro quo, solidify its position in Lebanon—and, indeed, all of these things occurred to a greater or lesser degree.

32. On the Arab cold war, see Malcolm Kerr's classic work, *The Arab Cold War: Gamal Abd al-Nasir and His Rivals, 1958–1970* (New York: Oxford University Press, 1971). Also see Fawaz A. Gerges, *The Superpowers and the Middle East: Regional and International Politics, 1955–1967* (Boulder: Westview Press, 1994). On the Syrian-Iraqi relationship, see Malik Mufti, *Sovereign Creations: Pan-Arabism and Political Order in Syria and Iraq* (Ithaca: Cornell University Press, 1996).

33. Ghassan Salame, "Inter-Arab Politics: The Return of Geography," in *The Middle East: Ten Years After Camp David,* ed. William B. Quandt (Washington, D.C.: Brookings Institution, 1988), p. 332. See also David W. Lesch, "Flanks, Balances, and Withdrawals: The Parameters of Syrian Policy in the Middle East Since the 1979 Egyptian-Israeli Peace Treaty," in *The Middle East Enters the 21st Century,* ed. Robert O. Freedman (forthcoming).

34. Ibid., pp. 322–323. Salame adds that in addition to the GCC led by Saudi Arabia, and the Levant trying to be led by Syria, the North African states had been relatively "neutralized" in inter-Arab affairs after displaying considerable

influence, especially Morocco and Algeria, in the early to mid-1970s. Part of the reason for this was the eruption of the Western Sahara issue in 1975, which pitted Morocco against Algeria, and Libya's growing maverick behavior (Salome, "Inter-Arab Politics" pp. 336–338). In addition, in my opinion, Egypt acted as not only a geographical bridge between the Maghrib (the "western" Arab states, that is, North Africa) and the Mashriq (or Arab East, which may or may not include Egypt) but also a political one, something of a conduit into mainstream Arab affairs. One must remember that Nasser touted Egypt as the link or center of three concentric circles: the Middle East, Africa, and the Islamic world. After the peace, the Egyptian link was severed.

35. Saddam also delivered the opening address at the Arab League summit meeting in Tunis on November 20, 1979.

36. Interestingly, in May 1979 Begin had proposed that Lebanese President Ilyas Sarkis meet with him to discuss the "signing of a peace treaty between Israel and Lebanon." Although the Lebanese rejected the proposal, this may have been the first public instance of the Begin government focusing on Lebanon in the aftermath of the peace treaty with Egypt, presaging a similar attempt, by a different methodology, in 1982. Also in 1979, in April, Lebanese Christian militia leader Colonel Sa'd Haddad met with Israeli Defense Minister Ezer Weizman, and soon after he announced the creation of an independent "Free Lebanon" in south Lebanon under the control of Christian militias. The foundation for the South Lebanese Army (SLA), a mostly Christian army initially under Haddad's command, was thus being laid, and it would remain allied to Israel all the way until its dissolution upon Israel's unilateral withdrawal from Lebanon in 2000.

37. The multinational effort can be divided into two parts, the one relatively successful, the other a disaster. Multinational Force I (MNF I) had the well-defined goal of escorting the PLO out of Beirut, with a clear exit strategy; this was viewed as a success. The chaos in Lebanon that followed the September 1982 assassination of Lebanese President Bashir Gemayel and the subsequent Phalangist retribution against Palestinians at the Sabra and Shatila refugee camps compelled, in a knee-jerk reaction, the multinational force to re-enter Beirut (MNF II) under the rather undefined rubric of somehow restoring stability and order in Lebanon. It was this ambiguous objective, with no clear exit strategy, that helped create the environment for the disasters that would soon befall MNF II and its eventual retreat from Lebanon by early 1984. See Anthony McDermott and Kjell Skjelsbaek, eds., *The Multinational Force in Beirut, 1982–1984* (Miami: Florida International University Press, 1991).

38. For instance, a former Egyptian defense minister, Abd al-Halim Abu Ghazala, who also served President Hosni Mubarak as an adviser until 1993, stated the following: "Peace with Israel is impossible. The peace we refer to is the just and stable peace that is rejected by Israel, which finds shelter in its arsenal of weapons of mass destruction and in the unconcealed American protection it receives. However, we should not be intimidated by this. Experience shows that we are capable of defeating it. The [Israeli] nuclear threat can be neutralized if the Arab states, especially those bordering Israel, succeed in

obtaining weapons capable of striking the Israeli depth, causing significant casualties and damage." *Middle East Newsline,* July 18, 2000,

39. Saad Eddin Ibrahim, "Domestic Developments in Egypt," in *The Middle East: Ten Years After Camp David,* ed. William B. Quandt (Washington, D.C.: Brookings Institution, 1988), p. 60.

40. William B. Quandt, "Introduction," in *The Middle East: Ten Years After Camp David,* ed. William B. Quandt (Washington, D.C.: Brookings Institution, 1988), p. 5.

41. The so-called final status issues consisted of the following: border demarcations between Israel and a presumed independent Palestinian state; the disposition of the more than 3.6 million UN-registered Palestinian refugees; the Jewish settlements in the West Bank, Gaza Strip, and Arab East Jerusalem; water-sharing of scarce water resources; and the question of Jerusalem, that is, whether it would remain the undivided capital of Israel, or whether Arab East Jerusalem would become the capital of a new Palestinian state (as demanded by the PLO), or whether there would be some sort of complex sovereignty-sharing formula.

42. Interestingly, Hilde Henriksen Waage, deputy director of the Peace Research Institute in Oslo, Norway, in his report titled "Norwegians? Who Needs Norwegians?" commissioned by the Norwegian Department of Foreign Affairs in 2000 and presented in January 2001, asserts that Yasir Arafat first envisioned the idea of utilizing Oslo as an intermediary with Israel in 1979 following the Egyptian-Israeli peace treaty. Arafat reportedly saw Norway as a perfect choice since it had excellent relations with Israel, the United States, and the Palestinians. Reported in *Middle East Newsline,* January 10, 2001.

43. Officially, the accords were signed by representatives of the Soviet puppet government in Kabul and the Pakistani government. Conspicuous by their absence, and foreshadowing the internal Afghani conflict to come, were any representatives from the *mujahideen.* As J. L. Richardson noted, "The Accords were negotiated at arm's length between a government highly dependent on its superpower protector (some observers would insist that it was totally dependent) and a government which informally controlled the supply of arms to the *Mujahideen* but had limited influence over their actions and represented their interests only to a limited extent. The exclusion of the *Mujahideen* from the diplomatic process, of course, points to the principal anomaly of the Accords. To construct a parallel in the Vietnamese case one would have to envisage a third party, say China, negotiating on behalf of North Vietnam with the government of South Vietnam." J. L. Richardson, "Conclusions: Management of the Afghan Crisis," in *The Soviet Withdrawal from Afghanistan,* ed. Amin Saikal and William Maley (Cambridge: Cambridge University Press, 1989), p. 162.

44. An opinion poll taken in 1985 stated that only one in four of the Soviet adult urban population approved of Soviet policy in Afghanistan. William Maley, "The Geneva Accords of April 1988," in *The Soviet Withdrawal from Afghanistan,* ed. Amin Saikal and William Maley (Cambridge: Cambridge University Press, 1989), p. 15.

45. T. H. Rigby, "The Afghan Conflict and Soviet Domestic Politics," in *The Soviet Withdrawal from Afghanistan*, ed. Amin Saikal and William Maley (Cambridge: Cambridge University Press, 1989), p. 73.

46. See Georgiy Mirsky, "The Soviet Perception of the U.S. Threat," in *The Middle East and the United States: A Historical and Political Reassessment*, 2nd ed., David W. Lesch (Boulder: Westview Press, 1999), pp. 395–403. Mirsky was one of those Soviet academics warning the Kremlin, as he has been an advisor to several Soviet/Russian leaders and is one of Russia's most distinguished scholars. He states: "Even before the final collapse, there was a sea change in foreign policy. Anti-imperialism as a guideline disappeared; promoting socialism worldwide became a futile task. Diplomatic relations with Israel had to be restored. De-ideologization meant that our relations with the Arab world were no longer dictated by the commitment to leftist Arab regimes and the need to deny the United States the dominant role in the area" (p. 401).

47. Richard A. Falk, "The Afghanistan 'Settlement' and the Future of World Politics," in *The Soviet Withdrawal from Afghanistan*, ed. Amin Saikal and William Maley (Cambridge: Cambridge University Press, 1989), p. 144. However, as Mirsky comments, when Gorbachev "gave the green light to de-Stalinization, little did he think that very soon it would turn into de-Leninization and de-Bolshevization." Mirsky, "The Soviet Perception of the U.S. Threat," p. 401. On elements of the new political thinking, see Robert O. Freedman, *Moscow and the Middle East: Soviet Policy Since the Invasion of Afghanistan* (Cambridge: Cambridge University Press, 1991), p. 206.

48. Falk, "The Afghanistan 'Settlement,'" p. 152.

49. Ibid., pp. 144–145.

50. Freedman, *Moscow and the Middle East*, pp. 317–318.

51. Ibid., p. 318.

52. Ibid.

53. There are those who contend that the warming of relations between the two superpowers that characterized détente policy as carried forward by the Nixon administration actually began to unravel with the close confrontation at the end of the 1973 Arab-Israeli war, signaling a renewed cold war rivalry in the Third World, which reached its fruition in Afghanistan. See Janice Gross Stein, "Flawed Strategies and Missed Signals: Crisis Bargaining Between the Superpowers, October 1973," in *The Middle East and the United States: A Historical and Political Reassessment*, 2nd edition, ed. David W. Lesch (Boulder: Westview Press, 1999), pp. 204–226.

54. As Geoffrey Jukes states, "Abstention from direct involvement in conflicts that they could not be sure of winning, such as Korea and Vietnam, helped the Soviet armed forces to acquire in the eyes of potential adversaries, and perhaps also in their own, a reputation for great capability, based on the one hand upon their undoubted achievements in the Second World War, and on the other upon their sheer size and estimates of the scale and quality of their equipment. So when Soviet forces entered Afghanistan, non-communist governments initially took their ability to dominate it for granted, and drew far-reaching strategic conclusions about Soviet designs on Gulf oil resources or sea-borne oil traffic." Geoffrey Jukes, "The Soviet Armed Forces and the

Afghan War," in *The Soviet Withdrawal from Afghanistan*, ed. Amin Saikal and William Maley (Cambridge: Cambridge University Press, 1989), p. 82. As Jukes notes, however, Soviet armed forces were mainly prepared and trained to fight a more traditional war against the United States and its NATO allies and not the type of guerrilla and counterinsurgency warfare characteristic of the Afghani conflict (pp. 84–85). It also should be mentioned here that the Soviet invasion equally alarmed China, particularly so soon after the Soviet-backed Vietnamese invasion of Cambodia earlier in the year, who perceived the invasion as an attempt to encircle, if not isolate, Beijing.

55. For a text of the Carter Doctrine, see Appendix C. For other statements made by President Carter in reaction to the Soviet invasion, see Edward H. Judge and John W. Langdon, eds., *The Cold War: A History Through Documents* (Upper Saddle River, N.J.: Prentice Hall, 1999), pp. 198–206.

56. Gary Sick, "The United States in the Persian Gulf: From Twin Pillars to Dual Containment," in *The Middle East and the United States: A Historical and Political Reassessment*, 2nd ed., ed. David W. Lesch (Boulder: Westview Press, 1999), p. 280.

57. Ibid.

58. "Afghan Camps, Hidden in Hills, Stymied Soviet Attacks for Years," *New York Times*, August 24, 1998, p. A1.

59. Before the Soviet invasion, Washington had actually been quite displeased with events that had been transpiring in Pakistan, especially the lack of democratic processes. Indeed, after Zia al-Haq had former president Zulfikar Bhutto executed on April 4, 1979, the United States two days later announced it had canceled economic and military assistance to Pakistan after concluding that Islamabad was building a plant to produce weapons-grade enriched uranium. The invasion of Afghanistan, therefore, clearly reversed this trend, as mutual interests made for a much closer relationship between Washington and Islamabad.

60. The United States began to send Stinger and Blowpipe anti-aircraft missiles by mid–1986, which proved to be a turning point in *mujahideen* capabilities. According to one source, the Soviets lost 512 aircraft and helicopters between January and November 1987, a dramatic increase from the period prior to the arrival of the anti-missile weaponry. Maley, "The Geneva Accords of April 1988," p. 16, in *The Soviet Withdrawal from Afghanistan*.

61. The various Islamist groups did succeed in forming a loose coalition in May 1985 known as the Islamic Unity of Afghan Mujahideen, which, along with crucial American military aid by 1986, better coordinated and enabled *mujahideen* military activities against the Soviets.

62. As Olivier Roy stated in 1994, clearly presaging the rise of a group like the Taliban, "Toward the end of the 1980s, the failure of the Islamist revolutionary idea [as in Iran] brought about the drift of a revolutionary, political, Third World type of Islamism, incarnated in the Iranian revolution, toward a puritanical, preaching, populist, conservative neofundamentalism, financed until recently by Saudi Arabia but violently anti-Western, particularly since the end of the East-West confrontation has ceased to cast communism as a foil." Roy, *The Failure of Political Islam*, (Cambridge: Harvard Univ. P., 1989) p. 25.

63. The Taliban is primarily composed of Pushtun Afghanis. It emerged in late 1994 as a messianic movement made up of students *(taliban)* who had been studying in Islamic *madrasas* (religious schools) in Pakistan as refugees from the Soviet invasion. They adopted a corrupted form of Deobandism, a branch of Sunni Islam that arose in India to confront British colonialism. Pakistani Deobandis had established by then a political party in Pakistan called the Jamiat-al-Ulama-e-Islam (JUI), an extremist Islamist group that had an anti-American bent. The JUI attached itself to the alliance that brought Prime Minister Benazir Bhutto to power in 1993, thus bringing the party into mainstream politics. From there it increasingly established strong links with the Inter-Services Intelligence agency (ISI) and with numerous military officers, especially those brought in during the days of Zia al-Haq, who had systematically begun the fundamentalist upsurge (and as many contend, with the support of Washington, which did not mind seeing growing worldwide Islamist opposition to Soviet interests). The strength of the JUI has grown in recent years and has become intimately linked with the Pakistani confrontation with India over Kashmir. As a result, the Taliban has been strongly supported by the Pakistani government unwilling to break its links with the JUI or Taliban (as demanded by the Clinton administration), which lends it necessary legitimacy and popularity in the inflammatory issue of Kashmir and in other aspects of the tense relationship with India. See Ahmed Rashid, "The Taliban: Exporting Extremism," *Foreign Affairs* 78, no. 6 (November-December 1999): 22–35.

64. The identification of the perpetrators of the al-Khobar bombing is still pending. The Clinton administration, in response to the embassy bombings, launched a surprise cruise missile attack on August 20 against a suspected bin Laden base in Afghanistan. Apparently the primary target, bin Laden himself, had left the compound just before the missiles hit.

65. Rashid, "The Taliban: Exporting Extremism," pp. 22–23.

66. Ibid., p. 31.

67. As Rashid states, "The joint venture between the Taliban and the JUI, funded by Saudi Wahhabis and supported by the Pakistani ISI, has become an ever-expanding enterprise, seeking new markets in Central Asia and beyond" (Rashid, "The Taliban: Exporting Extremism," p. 27). With the abundance of new oil reserves being discovered in Central Asia, particularly in places such as Kazakhstan, Azerbaijan, and Kyrgyzstan, and being exploited by Western multinational oil corporations, oil politics has inevitably become intertwined with this rising threat of instability, which many argue just enhances the need for a more active and forward foreign policy by the West, led by Washington, toward the region—and not just focusing on Osama bin Laden.

68. As one of the commanders under Gulbuddin Hekmatyar, the head of the strongest coalition of Islamist parties during the Soviet occupation who eventually took over Kabul in the early nineties, stated in 1994, "The whole country is a university for jihad. . . . We have had Egyptians, Sudanese, Arabs, and other foreigners trained here as assassins." *New York Times*, August 24, 1998, p. A1.

69. Sumit Ganguly, "Pakistan's Never-Ending Story: Why the October Coup Was No Surprise," *Foreign Affairs* 79, no. 2 (March-April 2000): 2–7.

70. Rashid, "The Taliban: Exporting Extremism," p. 28.

71. In addition, as Rashid notes, the "Islamicization" of the Kashmiri conflict has "undermined both the Kashmiris' own demand for self-determination from India and Pakistan's bid to win international mediation of the dispute." And the longer the conflict is supported by Arab and Afghani recruits turning it into a "Taliban jihad," the more they lose world sympathy. Rashid, "The Taliban: Exporting Extremism," p. 28.

72. Associated Press report, *San Antonio Express-News*, August 10, 2000.

73. As a sign of this new phenomenon, I receive on-line daily reports on Middle East activities from a service in Israel called Middle East Newsline. More often than not, there is a daily report on some aspect of U.S.-Chinese relations regarding Beijing's exportation to what Washington calls "states of concern" of long-range missiles or technology that could be utilized in weapons of mass destruction, or discussions in Congress over concerns the United States has in general regarding Chinese policy. Afghanistan brought China straight into the Middle East.

74. Rashid, "The Taliban: Exporting Extremism," p. 33.

75. Ibid. Rashid notes that the opposition Northern Alliance also imposes a similar tax on opium production and shipments under its control.

76. Ibid., p. 34.

77. Ibid.

78. Ibid., p. 35.

79. Actually it was OAPEC (the Organization of Arab Exporting Petroleum Countries) that launched the embargo, that is, the Arab members of OPEC. The embargo was first placed upon the United States and the Netherlands; later added to the list were Rhodesia, Portugal, and South Africa. In addition, in November 1973, OAPEC announced a 25 percent reduction in production from the September 1973 levels.

80. Mohammed Abu Al Khail, "The Oil Price in Perspective," in *The Politics of Middle Eastern Oil*, ed. J. E. Peterson (Washington, D.C.: Middle East Institute, 1983), p. 72.

81. Ibid.

82. Dankwart A. Rustow, *Oil and Turmoil: America Faces OPEC and the Middle East* (New York: W. W. Norton, 1982), p. 183.

83. Ibid., p. 184.

Chapter 4

1. The Palestinian uprising began when Likud party leader Ariel Sharon, who is despised by Palestinians for his role in an attack on a Jordanian village in the 1950s and his role in the Sabra and Shatila massacres in 1982 in Lebanon, visited the Temple Mount, or Haram al-Sharif, one of the holiest sites in all of Islam, containing the Dome of the Rock and the al-Aqsa mosque, both of which were built in commemoration of the Prophet Muhammad's legendary night journey to heaven, and it is certainly *the* holiest site in all of Judaism, being the location of the destroyed First and Second Temples, origi-

nally constructed by Solomon and later rebuilt by Herod the Great. The Western Wall (or Wailing Wall) is all that remains of the Second Temple. Why Sharon made such a gesture in such a volatile atmosphere is left to speculation, but many suggest that by reasserting Israel's claim to all of Jerusalem Sharon was trying to solidify his position within Likud prior to probable new elections for prime minister (elections were indeed held in February 2001, and Sharon was elected prime minister in a landslide victory over Ehud Barak). The Palestinians, who were intensely frustrated by the failure of Camp David in July and indeed by the whole Oslo process, and possibly spurred on by the example of Hizbullah in southern Lebanon, cathartically vented their anger following the Sharon visit—an anger that most agree was exploited by Yasir Arafat to some degree in an attempt to solidify his political position and increase his negotiating leverage. There followed attacks by Palestinians on Israelis and Jewish sites and Israeli military countermeasures that most described as nothing less than a mini-war.

2. Underscoring this recognition, amid discussions between Egyptian and American officials concerning a free trade agreement between the two countries, House representatives in Congress sent a letter of support to President Clinton in which it was stated: "Egypt, one of America's most important Arab allies, is essential to our regional security interests. Egypt was the first Arab nation to conclude a peace agreement with Israel and is fundamental to moving peace negotiations forward between Israel, the Palestinians, and other Arab states." *Middle East Newsline,* November 6, 2000, p. 11.

3. On November 20, 2000, Egypt withdrew its ambassador to Israel in protest of a very intense Israeli military response against PNA targets in the Gaza Strip, following a Palestinian bomb attack against an Israeli school bus full of children the previous day.

4. As one scholar noted, "The overthrow of the Shah of Iran in 1979—seen by Muslims as a vindication of Islam against the corrupting influence of the West—was a watershed for Islamic activists. It demonstrated the vitality of Islamic political ideology as an independent force and inspired like-minded activists throughout the Muslim world. The successes in Afghanistan against the Soviet forces further strengthened the idea of Islam as a viable political ideology. Consequently, Islamic activists came to understand the political utility of religion and the effectiveness of using the mosque as a center of protest in countries where opposition was otherwise banned." Scott W. Hibbard and David Little, *Islamic Activism and U.S. Foreign Policy* (Washington, D.C.: United States Institute of Peace Press, 1997), p. 10.

5. Louis J. Cantori, "Sovereignty Is with God and His Khilafa Are the Ulama," *Muslim Democrat* 2, no. 1 (February 2000): p. 8.

6. *Middle East Newsline,* August 28, 2000.

7. Terrorist experts, however, point out that the timing of the attack on the USS *Cole* was only coincidental with the al-Aqsa *intifadah* since the general consensus is that the relatively sophisticated operation required at least several months of planning, probably beginning well before even the July 2000 Camp David summit. It is also interesting to note that Osama bin Laden's family is Saudi but of Yemeni origin and that Yemen was one of the leading

contributors in the Arab world, in terms of the number of volunteers, to the *mujahideen* war effort in Afghanistan.

8. The term "crossing" has reverential connotations within Egypt. It refers to what in the Egyptian view was the almost miraculous military crossing of the Suez Canal at the beginning of the 1973 Arab-Israeli war amid heavy Israeli artillery fire from the Israeli-controlled east bank of the canal. The audacious operation was successful and preceded the establishment of the Egyptian bridgehead on the east bank. It is known in Egypt simply as "The Crossing" and is celebrated every year in on October 6, the day when the military operation was launched in 1973. Ironically, it was also the day that Anwar Sadat was assassinated by Islamic extremists in 1981 amid the annual ceremonial pageantry commemorating the event

BIBLIOGRAPHY

History and Annualization

Ankersmit, Frank, and Hans Kellner, eds. *A New Philosophy of History.* Chicago: University of Chicago Press, 1995.

Bender, Thomas. "Wholes and Parts: The Need for Synthesis in American History." *Journal of American History* 73, no. 1 (June 1986): 120–136.

Brewer, John. "The Year of Writing Dangerously." *New Republic* (August 3, 1998): 42–45.

Brook-Shepard, Gordon. *November 1918.* Boston: Little, Brown, 1981.

Cameron, James. *1914.* Westport, Conn.: Greenwood Press, 1975.

Carrard, Philippe. "To Tell or Not to Tell: The New History and the Rebirth of Narrative." *French Forum* 14, no. 2 (May 1989): 219–227.

Chandler, James. *England in 1819: The Politics of Literary Culture and the Case of Romantic Historicism.* Chicago: University of Chicago Press, 1998.

Collier, Richard. *1940: The Avalanche.* New York: Dial Press, 1979.

Cowles, Virginia. *1913: An End and a Beginning.* New York: Harper and Row, 1967.

Dowling, William C. *Jameson, Althusser, Marx: An Introduction to the Political Unconscious.* Ithaca: Cornell University Press, 1984.

Elton, G. R. *Political History: Principles and Practice.* New York: Basic Books, 1970.

Fleming, Thomas. *1776: Year of Illusions.* New York: W. W. Norton, 1975.

Furet, François. *In the Workshop of History.* Translated by Jonathan Mandelbaum. Chicago: University of Chicago Press, 1984.

Geiss, Imanuel, ed. *July 1914: The Outbreak of the First World War.* New York: W. W. Norton, 1967.

Gilbert, Felix, and Stephen R. Graubard, eds. *Historical Studies Today.* New York: W. W. Norton, 1972.

Gilpin, Robert. *War and Change in World Politics.* Cambridge: Cambridge University Press, 1981.

Herubel, Jean-Pierre V. M., comp. *Annales Historiography and Theory: A Selective and Annotated Bibliography*. Westport, Conn.: Greenwood Press, 1994.

Hodgen, Margaret T. *Change and History: A Study of the Dated Distributions of Technological Innovations in England*. New York: Wenner-Gren Foundations for Anthropological Research, 1952.

Huang, Ray. *1587, A Year of No Significance: The Ming Dynasty in Decline*. New Haven: Yale University Press, 1981.

Kegley, Charles W., Jr, Gregory A. Raymond, Robert M. Rood, and Richard A Skinner, eds. *International Events and the Comparative Analysis of Foreign Policy*. Columbia: University of South Carolina Press, 1975.

Klingaman, William K. *1941: Our Lives in a World on the Edge*. New York: Harper and Row, 1988.

Lévi-Strauss, Claude. *The Savage Mind*. Chicago: University of Chicago Press, 1962.

Lombard, Lawrence Brian. *Events: A Metaphysical Study*. London: Routledge and Kegan Paul, 1986.

Ludwig, Emil. *July '14*. Translated by C. A. Macartney. New York: G. P. Putnam's Sons, 1929.

Macdonald, Lyn. *1914*. New York: Atheneum Macmillan, 1987.

Macdonald, Lyn. *1915: The Death of Innocence*. New York: Henry Holt, 1993.

Maoz, Zeev. *Domestic Sources of Global Change*. Ann Arbor: University of Michigan Press, 1996.

Marx, Karl. *The Eighteenth Brumaire of Louis Bonaparte*. New York: International, 1972.

Munz, Peter. *The Shapes of Time: A New Look at the Philosophy of History*. Middletown, Conn.: Wesleyan University Press, 1977.

Oakeshott, Michael. *Experience and Its Modes*. Cambridge: Cambridge University Press, 1933.

Oakeshott, Michael. *On History: And Other Essays*. Oxford: Basil Blackwell, 1983.

Phelan, James, ed. *Reading Narrative: Form, Ethics, Ideology*. Columbus: Ohio State University Press, 1989.

Renier, Gustaaf Johannes. *History: Its Purpose and Method*. Macon, Georgia: Mercer University Press, 1950.

Stanford, Michael. *Introduction to the Philosophy of History*. Cambridge: Blackwell, 1998.

Starobinski, Jean. *1789: The Emblems of Reason*. London: MIT Press, 1988.

Stone, Lawrence. "The Revival of Narrative: Reflections on a New Old History." *Past and Present* 85 (November 1979): 3–24.

Teggart, Frederick J. *Theory and Processes of History*. Berkeley: University of California Press, 1960.

Walsh, W. H. *An Introduction to Philosophy of History*. New Jersey: Humanities Press, 1967.

Weber, Max. *The Theory of Social and Economic Organization*. Edited by A. M. Henderson and Talcott Parsons. New York: Oxford University Press, 1947.

The Iranian Revolution

Amirahmadi, Hooshang, and Nadar Entessar, eds. *Iran and the Arab World.* New York: St. Martin's Press, 1993.

Bakhash, Shaul. *The Reign of the Ayatollahs: Iran and the Islamic Revolution.* New York: Basic Books, 1984.

Freedman, Lawrence, and Efraim Karsh. *The Gulf Conflict, 1990–1991: Diplomacy and War in the New World Order.* Princeton: Princeton University Press, 1993.

Halliday, Fred. *Islam and the Myth of Confrontation: Religion and Politics in the Middle East.* London: I. B. Tauris, 1995.

Hume, Cameron R. *The United Nations, Iran, and Iraq: How Peacemaking Changed.* Bloomington: Indiana University Press, 1994.

Keddie, Nikki R. *Roots of Revolution: An Interpretive History of Modern Iran.* New Haven: Yale University Press, 1981.

Khomeini, Imam. *Islam and Revolution.* Translated by Hamid Algar. Berkeley: Mizan Press, 1981.

King, Ralph. "The Iran-Iraq War: The Political Implications," *Adephi Papers* 219, Spring 1987.

Lesch, David W., ed. *The Middle East and the United States: A Historical and Political Reassessment,* 2nd ed. Boulder: Westview Press, 1999.

Milani, Mohsen M. *The Making of Iran's Islamic Revolution: From Monarchy to Islamic Republic.* Boulder: Westview Press, 1994.

Mottahedeh, Roy. *The Mantle of the Prophet: Religion and Politics in Iran.* New York: Pantheon Books, 1985.

Parsa, Misagh. *Social Origin of the Iranian Revolution.* New Brunswick: Rutgers University Press, 1989.

Peterson, J. E., ed. *The Politics of Middle Eastern Oil.* Washington, D.C.: Middle East Institute, 1983.

Quandt, William B. *Saudi Arabia in the 1980s: Foreign Policy, Security, and Oil.* Washington, D.C.: Brookings Institution, 1981.

Ramazani, R. K., ed. *Iran's Revolution: The Search for Consensus.* Bloomington: Indiana University Press, 1990.

Rubin, Barry. *Paved with Good Intentions: The American Experience and Iran.* New York: Penguin Books, 1982.

Rustow, Dankwart A. *Oil and Turmoil: America Faces OPEC and the Middle East.* New York: W. W. Norton, 1982.

Shawcross, William. *The Shah's Last Ride: The Fate of an Ally.* New York: Simon and Schuster, 1988.

Sick, Gary. *All Fall Down: America's Tragic Encounter with Iran.* New York: Penguin Books, 1986.

U.S. News & World Report. *Triumph Without Victory: The History of the Persian Gulf War.* New York: Times Books, 1993.

Voll, John Obert. *Islam: Continuity and Change in the Modern World.* Boulder: Westview Press, 1982.

Yetiv, Steve. *Fateful Decisions: Explaining the Last Major Middle East Crisis of the 20th Century.* Unpublished manuscript.

Zahlan, Rosemarie Said. *The Making of the Modern Gulf States*. London: Ithaca Press, 1998.

The Egyptian-Israeli Peace Treaty

Bickerton, Ian J., and Carla L. Klausner. *A Concise History of the Arab-Israeli Conflict*. Upper Saddle River, N.J.: Prentice Hall, 1998.

Freedman, Robert O., ed. *The Middle East Since Camp David*. Boulder: Westview Press, 1984.

Freedman, Robert O., ed. *The Middle East After the Israeli Invasion of Lebanon*. Syracuse, N.Y.: Syracuse University Press, 1986.

Jureidini, Paul A., and R. D. McLaurin. *Beyond Camp David: Emerging Alignments and Leaders in the Middle East*. Syracuse, N.Y.: Syracuse University Press, 1981.

Khouri, Fred J. *The Arab-Israeli Dilemma*, 3rd ed. Syracuse, N.Y.: Syracuse University Press, 1985.

Lesch, David W., ed. *The Middle East and the United States: A Historical and Political Reassessment*, 2nd ed. Boulder: Westview Press, 1999.

Lorenz, Joseph P. *Egypt and the Arabs: Foreign Policy and the Search for National Identity*. Oxford: Westview Press, 1990.

Quandt, William B. *Camp David: Peacemaking and Politics*. Washington, D.C.: Brookings Institution, 1986.

Quandt, William B. *Decade of Decisions: American Policy Toward the Arab-Israeli Conflict, 1967–1976*. Berkeley: University of California Press, 1977.

Quandt, William B. *Peace Process: American Diplomacy and the Arab-Israeli Conflict Since 1967*. Berkeley: University of California Press, 1993.

Quandt, William B., ed. *The Middle East: Ten Years After Camp David*. Washington, D.C.: Brookings Institution, 1988.

Rabinovich, Itamar. *The War for Lebanon, 1970–1985*. Ithaca: Cornell University Press, 1985.

Reich, Bernard, ed. *Arab-Israeli Conflict and Conciliation: A Documentary History*. Westport, Conn.: Praeger, 1995.

Safran, Nadav. *Israel: The Embattled Ally*. Cambridge: Belknap Press of Harvard University Press, 1982.

Smith, Charles D. *Palestine and the Arab-Israeli Conflict*. New York: St. Martin's Press, 2001.

Spiegel, Steven L. *The Other Arab-Israeli Conflict: Making America's Middle East Policy, from Truman to Reagan*. Chicago: University of Chicago Press, 1985.

Stein, Kenneth W. *Heroic Diplomacy: Sadat, Kissinger, Carter, Begin, and the Quest*. New York: Routledge, 1999.

The Soviet Invasion of Afghanistan

Arnold, Anthony. *Afghanistan: The Soviet Invasion in Perspective*. Stanford: Hoover Institution Press, 1985.

Freedman, Robert O. *Moscow and the Middle East: Soviet Policy Since the Invasion of Afghanistan.* Cambridge: Cambridge University Press, 1991.

Ganguly, Sumit. "Pakistan's Never-ending Story: Why the October Coup Was No Surprise." *Foreign Affairs* 79, no. 2 (March-April 2000): 2–7.

Hammond, Thomas T. *Red Flag over Afghanistan: The Communist Coup, the Soviet Invasion, and the Consequences.* Boulder: Westview Press, 1984.

Kakar, M. Hassan. *Afghanistan: The Soviet Invasion and the Afghan Response, 1979–1982.* Berkeley: University of California Press, 1995.

Mandelbaum, Michael, ed. *Central Asia and the World.* New York: Council on Foreign Relations Press, 1994.

Rashid, Ahmed. "The Taliban: Exporting Extremism." *Foreign Affairs* 78, no. 6 (November-December 1999): 22–35.

Roy, Olivier. *The Failure of Political Islam.* Translated by Carol Volk. Cambridge: Harvard University Press, 1994.

Saikal, Amin, and William Maley, eds. *The Soviet Withdrawal from Afghanistan.* New York: Cambridge University Press, 1989.

INDEX